WELCOME to Boulevard Books –
new authors,
new translations
new experiences.

Sandra Petrignani explores the
sensuality, excitement and sadness
toys and games hold for children and
succeeds in stirring up deep and
pleasureable adult memories in her
funny, *simpatico* book 'The Toy
Catalogue'. This is the first in the
'Boulevard Italians' series of
contemporary fiction from Europe's
most creative young writers.

The Toy Catalogue

Sandra
Petrignani

Translated by Ray Lombardo

BOULEVARD

THE TOY CATALOGUE

First published as 'Il Catalogo dei Giocattoli'
copyright ©1988 Edizioni Theoria s.r.l., Roma-Napoli.

Translation copyright © 1990 Boulevard Books.
First published 1990 by Boulevard Books
14 Lomley House, Tulse Hill, London SW2 2EW

The publishers wish to thank Jean-Luc Barbanneau, Fiorenza Conte,
Laura Grandi and Nuova Immagine Siena for their help in
establishing the Boulevard Italians series.

The translator thanks Dr. Sharon Wood, Pamm Flores and Gareth
Stanton for their assistance and would like to dedicate the translation
with love and gratitude to the memory of Anne K.

ISBN 0 946889 23 6

Boulevard Books are published in the UK in association with Olive
Press/Impact Books and distributed by the Harraps Publishing Group.

Cover art by Phil Baines & Tenné Vair.

Typeset by Saxon, Derby.

Printed and bound by the Guernsey Press, Guernsey, C.I.

contents

abacus

We never thought it was any use for adding up.

You could get the coloured wooden balls to spin giddily around their metal rods. They made a racket like an engine starting. Roll the balls under your palm and you got a tender caress, a massage.

Eventually the rods would break away from the frame. The balls tumble one after the other onto the floor, tinkling like the pearls from a broken necklace. And who knows how, who knows where, but one would disappear for good; not even the most thorough search could flush it out again. And that was just when you wanted to use the abacus to add up with, to learn to do what you never wanted to do when there was nothing to stop you from doing it.

There were those grey days, when it was foggy or it was raining, opening the shutters or keeping them closed, it didn't make any difference. And the electric light projected elongated shadows which made you see yourself in grown-up proportions. In the house could be heard the sad, lonely rattle of the abacus in a child's hands being shaken from right to left and left to right as the little balls rolled relentlessly from side to side.

baby doll

The baby doll, because it's a newborn baby and not a fake toddler or a toddler pretending to be a grown up, is one of the most worthwhile of all toys. It was being made from a pliable plastic as early as the 1950's and this material was its main source of attraction. But softness has always been one of its features and even before this plastic was developed only the limbs and the head were of hard material grafted on to a cloth torso. This type of construction has come back into fashion recently, the only difference being the use of plastic instead of bisque porcelain and celluloid. The arms, legs and rounded head hang loosely from the stuffed body. The smell is immensely important. The soft plastic it's made from has a rather special fragrance which, although different for different sorts, is completely irresistible. Many years ago there was a particular doll which had a scent of talc and flowers reminiscent of certain perfumes. Delving into a woman's past one might discover some relationship between the perfume she chooses as an adult and the doll she played with when she was little.

There was a fascinating uncertainty about the gender of these toys. The whim of little girls was that they were male. Nowadays baby dolls have little organs sculpted out of plastic, a little trench that runs along a slight swelling for the females, a sort of snail-thing for the males. Small girls are captivated by this snail which brings back over-whelming memories of the nipple and they instinctively take it into their mouths to suck on. An awful thing about the baby doll was its voice. It had a little round box in its belly with a tiny bellows hidden inside it. If one turned the toy upside- down and back again rapidly, the bellows would slide down the cylinder and the movement of air produced a noise supposed to be the word 'mama'. It was more like an anguished wail or animal cry. This haunting little tune issued from an aperture in the middle of the stomach disguised as a belly button. In some models the voice box could be removed quite easily, and often became a separate toy which kids would play with by turning it over and over in their hands. The baby doll was then left in a mutilated condition and one could put all kinds of little objects – pebbles, dice, scraps of cloth, pearls – into the perfectly circular hole opening on to its intestinal cavity. Anything would do to fill this repugnant gap – in itself a very good reason to prefer the soft fullness of the teddy bear and other toys made from fabric or fur. But one couldn't deny there were also some advantages to be had from this empty space. Some baby dolls were equipped to do a pee-pee. There was a little hole between their lips which connected up with another hole between their legs. You gave them a feeding bottle with water or milk to drink and the liquid would drain out underneath to the great mirth of all those present.

One day a baby doll ended up in the fish tank which left a lasting impression of the fish darting away terrified, air bubbles of someone drowning and that distant, un-changing expression that a foetus wears as it spins blind somersaults through the prenatal fluid. It's not quite right to say that baby dolls simulate newborns; their true model is the baby just before birth.

It must have seemed a very macabre game to the woman on the ground floor. We hung two naked dolls on long strings and made them swing back and forth in front of her window. We jerked them about from overhead like puppets. It didn't last long – snip, snip. She had cut the threads and the dolls were lost.

'bagatelle' or table football

The sound of the balls raining down into their container. The sound a ball makes rolling between the legs of a footballer-on-a-stick. The sound a ball makes going into a goal and the joyful cry of the one who scored, the groan of the one who didn't manage to defend. One put fifty *lira* into the slot of the 'bagatelle' (nobody ever called it by its official name of *Calciobalilla* from *Calcio*, football and *Balilla*, a fascist youth organization, maybe because it reminded our parents of their childhood under fascism and they avoided the term). You pulled hard on the piston and the balls began to drop into the tray outside. You checked to see that all ten were there and that one wasn't trapped inside, caught up in the gears of the machinery. If that happened you had to lift the table up on one side by holding onto the lever and shake it until the tardy ball found its way out to come down and join its comrades. Then you could release the handle and the drawer went back into position with a 'clack'. The balls looked as if they had been formed out of a heavy wax, white with little black dust spots imprisoned in the whiteness. The concerto of rumbles and reverberations, the odd consistency of the balls, the heaviness of the table, the puppets dressed as footballers, the metal bars, the greasy handles, all made the barroom bagatelle far superior to the household model which arrived one Christmas to keep your brothers happy. You used the little home model as a makeshift or to get some practice or when it was raining and you weren't allowed out. Or at night before bedtime. It was always available, you didn't have to queue up to use it or spend any money. But there was no honour in that. The bar game on the other hand had all the seriousness of real life and accomplished playing would attract spectators and admiration too. There were long discussions about the validity of certain goals. And the skillfulness of a little girl amidst a group of boys bigger than herself did not go entirely without notice.

ball

Nausicaa was playing a ball game with her handmaids when she met Ulysses. They were playing with the 'heavenly sphere' which stood for the sun or the moon and which they threw up to the sky one by one as they danced along. The springy bouncing of a rubber ball – a pleasurable sound that harks back to our childhood. It's the first of the world's shapes to be recognised from the cradle, the first plaything which isn't just a rattle or a soft toy. Inexperienced hands venture right around the smooth shape, pushing and poking it when they learn how, and discovering that this thing knows how to roll about, can hide itself under the furniture, disappear from view, melt away. And just like the sun it comes up and goes down.

The ball is the most adaptable of all toys; suitable for team play or when you're on your own. The noise it makes bouncing back is light and peaceful and there's an almost infinite number of ways to use it. Football, circle or throwing-and- jumping games, Dodge Ball, Touch Ball, Poison Ball. Throwing it against a wall is generally done when you're on your own: you throw it to yourself against a free wall and recite a nonsense-rhyme (...onesy twosy pick-and-choosey threesy foursy winsy-losey...). It's a game of skill that the girls excel at because of their stubborn determination to get better at it; because of the grace with which they can spin a pirouette in the fraction of a moment it takes for the ball to bounce back from the wall. And they nimbly lift a leg to throw the coloured sphere under the arc of the knee and turn and fling it behind them or between their thighs, catching it again after patting it once or twice with the hand. Playing with a ball was a favourite with little girls who lived in houses with inside courtyards, those communal gardens where it was permissible to use the wall of the house for throwing a rubber ball. The boys preferred open spaces. They often played quite undisturbed in the street: there weren't any parked cars and the pavements were empty, you could hear bicycles ring their bells from a long way off and cars were infrequent and drove slowly. And when they did appear everyone would get out of the way together, all sweaty, the ball under someone's arm, to let them pass and one would hang on for a bit to have a breather, taking advantage of the interruption.

The air had a freshness about it. Winter was barely over and you tried to make the day last into the blue borders of the night, disputing eventide with the mothers who at the first darkening would stick their heads out of the windows and shrilly call you in. One by one the little boys would go off home with the boundless sadness of dwarves in the Land of the Giants.

balloons

There's a song that goes *Dove vanno a finire i palloncini/ quando sfuggono alle mani dei bambini?* ('Where do the balloons end up/ when they fly from the hands of children?'). Unlike the souls of the departed which hover near graveyards or next to candles that flicker before their portraits, balloons just fly away. They go off to discover if angels are for real, snatching from the despairing child some of his already limited power over objects, his life and other people.

It was always very tiresome the way the grownups wanted to tie the string around your wrist, anxious to convince you that this was the ideal system, applying their usual unyielding logic. All you needed to do was hold the string and keep it taut the whole time. The balloon would pull away giving you this strange sensation of anti-weight, weight that wanted to rise rather than fall. And then the inevitable would happen, the moment when the string would shoot off unexpectedly; just an instant of distraction, the tiniest slackening and the string was away leaving the minutest trace of its presence on your sweaty palm. And this was when the grownup would say 'There, I told you so.' and the child, stricken with astonishment, would turn his face up to follow that mysterious progress across the skies and straightaway he wanted another balloon. This time he'd allow it to be tied to his wrist and he'd look at his new acquisition, at once cheered up and ashamed, sensing the mischievous delight of the first balloon up above him almost as if it were sitting on a cloud looking down and sneering at him rather pleased with its amazing escape.

The captive balloon would be brought home like a trophy. As soon as it was let loose it would hurl itself up to the ceiling where the child, rather cross, couldn't get at it. Then it would be tied to an extra-long string and could be caught with a leap or held down by attaching some little weights to it (but it would wriggle half-way up again). When you felt like it you could squeeze it at the bottom, gripping it between your palms to feel its lightness and warmth. The day after it would take twice as long to get up to the ceiling and would come down quietly and obediently with the slightest tug on the string. The day after that it would waver about the room like a drunk, responding listlessly to the little taps intended to relaunch it, then settle all puckered-up on the floor. It had become, as was its natural fate, a deflated balloon. It could now only dance docilely on your fingers, tap pianissimo against your head, giving you all the time in the world to catch it again after a torpid flight. But one of its delirium-inducing features remained: the smell. Even when popped, or if it suddenly and inexplicably burst, it kept in each shred – children would barbarically rip it up – that strong smell of sulphur, of ravished intimacy, of incense. And its fragments weren't thrown away but moved from one toy-box to another or carried in the mouth and sucked on as a novel type of chewing gum, or stretched out as far as they would go. Then the pieces would finally disappear, perhaps through the agency of adults in the name of tidying-up or through that everyday wear and tear that uses up and obliterates all things.

barbie

She came crashing into the lives of little girls born in the early 1950's and teetering on the brink of adolescence. Girls who'd seen 'Gone with the Wind' and Marlene Dietrich's films and were pondering at the crossroads between maternal prototype and seductive vamp. Barbie was beautiful, wealthy and independent. She possessed various gadgets, clothes, and at least one man, her fiancé Ken. And she had a whole set of friends. She obviously had some up-to-the-minute career: model-girl, journalist or film actress. Her wardrobe suggested trips abroad, responsibilities, elegant evenings out. Buying Barbie a new outfit with your weekly pocket money meant earning an advance on your own future autonomy, it was a kind of trial run, a peep into the future. Barbie wasn't a doll, she was an aspiration. Invented by the unwitting genius of some – probably unknown – toymaker, she went on to fire the disobedient dreams of a generation that would challenge, burn, love freely and then enter with dynamism and creativity into high-class career environments. Barbie had jeans and designer suits, a bicycle and a sports car. Beauty and elegance were a game and an achievement, not the essential starting point to get ahead. She didn't seem to have a family and pregnancy wouldn't suit her figure. She was just old enough to have had the chance to establish her future, to have her own place to live in and her own style.

When she was born in '59, and for the next few years, Barbie was the only one of her kind. The only choice you had was over her hair colour – blonde, brunette or redhead. Now there are many sorts of Barbies and out of this proliferation the conventional feminine split, emancipated woman versus angel of the hearth, has re-emerged. A girl's focus has been shifted from the single object to the collection, her fantasies harnessed to stereotypes. There's Barbie the housewife, sporty Barbie, Barbie the top model and Barbie the mother, with rounded tummy and her little one by her side. This one is the most progressive version of the standard Barbie.

bicycle

First there's the tricycle - it's bright red, safe and comfortable to use. There's the feeling of growing up on it, the pleasure of getting bigger while the plaything becomes small. And you stick your knees out sideways so they don't get in the way of the handlebars. And you push the pedals around with maniacal joy. The next stage is the bike with training wheels on the side. A taste of instability which gets harder to deal with when one of the wheels is taken off. To pedal becomes to tremble. The strain of those beginning ventures on three wheels. With that first grownups' machine a kid senses the great responsibility of being a living creature, a true inhabitant of the world.

There is a certain point in the journey from childhood to adolescence where you encounter a dangerous pass, an ordeal to endure before you can win the kingdom. This point is the day you manage to stay in the saddle when the second training wheel is unhooked. A youthful father keeps a hand on the saddle as he follows the bike on foot and murmurs words of encouragement to his daughter who is pedalling gingerly away. She doesn't realize it but now and again he checks the little girl's balance by letting go his grip for a few seconds. When he's sure she can do it he warns her 'Okay I'm letting go, go by yourself.' She squeals excitedly, 'No, not yet, no don't!' like when she's getting an injection and wants to delay the needle going in. But it's already happened, she's running free, flying solo, away on two wheels. Daddy stops to watch her; he's caught between jubilation and pathos.

The little girl doesn't remember learning to walk but she knows she must have felt something like this new dignity, this justifiable pride. The bicycle is one of the few things that run right through people's lives from infancy to maturity without humiliating distinctions based on age. Everyone can go cycling together and it can happen that the youngest is the one who's most deft and daring. The more you practice the more skillful you become and the more tricks you can do. The first one is taking a hand off the handlebars and ringing frenetically on the bell. Then tearing down the hill without braking, then pedalling while standing up, then with no hands, then on just one pedal, then leaping off the saddle while the bike's still moving as you come home from school, starving, shoving the bike into the garage and hurriedly slinging your books onto the hall table to get to dinner on time. At this stage the bicycle has become an extension of the body, of the legs and hands, thereby adding a quadruped's equilibrium to the tiresome perpendicularity of our human state.

A little note in the margin: the bicycle is sexed, existing in male and female forms. The boy's version with its crossbar running from saddle to handlebars is more uncomfortable than the girls' version; and if we were restricted to just one kind, without a doubt the more rational choice would be the one without the crossbar. Nevertheless the crossbar has its charm. It used to be the place to carry one's beloved. Or where big brothers would take their little sisters for a ride.

The workers of the city of Piacenza would pedal through the mist to the arsenal with their shapeless black or brown leather tradesman's bags suspended from the crossbar. They'd thread the drawstring through the metal tubing, wrap it securely round the bar, and the bike's motion would make the bag swing gently to and fro. They didn't keep paperwork in these bags but their lunchtime provisions, bread and an omelette, bread and meat, a bottle of wine.

blackboards and magic slates

Someone always ended up behind the blackboard. You could see a pair of ashamed naked legs below it. The class monitor would write the names of the good and bad students up on the blackboard which was divided in two by a line drawn down the middle. With a quick flash of the board wiper and a flick of the chalk good students would get moved over to the bad student column – but hardly ever the other way around. Notwithstanding, the blackboard, with its literal name and its largish form, was thought of as a toy, even there in the classroom. It was a Queen amongst toys, the heart of the classroom in the days when classrooms were big and you could run about and chase each other around the blackboard. Sentences and numbers all in white settled powdery on a cold black sea. Words became things; temporary corporeal forms. Up there all mistakes were corrected and no disgraceful marks were left behind because they just dispersed into a hovering cloud which sifted itself shapelessly into your hair and the pores of your skin, making your fingers stiff and heavy. The chalks were long. Dividing them up was a special treat because of the feeling of responsibility one got. You had to break them exactly in the middle with a dry snap. Otherwise the longer bit would scratch on the board causing everybody to hunch up and grit their teeth.

On the little slate at home you made obscene pictures you'd quickly rub out after showing them to your sisters or smaller brothers. The pictures were scatological obscenities and produced a feeling of disgust mixed with excitement. These little slates were never used for serious study. They weren't big enough to do sums on and they were too temporary to record thoughts on. And then the 'magic' sort came along, thin, clean, modern, capable of recording every mark made by the pen and erasing it quickly with a rod moved across the two waxed sheets. But it wasn't as if some long-awaited need had been fulfilled. The two blackboards happily coexisted – if one emphasizes that, in a child's mind, the black one definitely belonged to the world of toys.

bottle tops

Crown caps from Campari, Coca-Cola and orangeade ended up in a shoe box, individually wrapped in the silver and gold tinfoil from sweets and chocolates. They looked like coins. You shook the box to feel their weight and hear them scrape about across the bottom. More than anything you had them for the pleasure of making a collection, they differed from each other only by virtue of belonging to the golds or the silvers. You really needed a lot of them – all you could pick up from the table after lunch or from the counter or the floor of the bar. But you could also play with them like marbles, flicking them with a scratching sound along a defined track, silvers against golds. For these competitions the sweet wrappers were removed and smoothed out with the hands until they lost all their creases.

The little girls would use the same tinfoil to make imitations of their mothers' wedding rings. Then they would try and slip them onto the fingers of unwilling males. Especially prized was the shiny red transparent paper from Rossana toffees. First you'd smooth it out like the tinfoil then, squinting an eye and pulling a face, you'd look at the world through it. Grasping the edges with two fists and scrunching it back and forth, pushing it and pulling it apart, it crackled in a way that delighted the untrained ear of a child but drove the adult sensibility to distraction.

bucket and spade

The complete kit for going to the beach comprised an inflatable beach ball with coloured segments, a bucket, a spade, a rake, a sieve, moulds, a watering-can, a wheelbarrow. The moulds were in the shapes of sea shells, fish, starfish and pies, which could be oval, round or rectangular. You filled them up with damp sand smoothed down around the edges by patting and scraping with the palm of the hand, then they were laid onto beaten-down sand and tapped around the sides. One gently raised the mould, which left a perfect impression on the shaped sand. If you were lucky that's what happened – which it rarely did. Usually the sand was either too dry or too wet and the mould wouldn't come away completely. So the shapes would be a bit mutilated – the fish with no tail, the starfish with only one of its arms – and this left one feeling slightly sad and mildly disappointed. Even the bucket could be used as a large mould on occasion, serving to raise the four turrets of a sandcastle. Bucket materials changed as time wore on, going from enamelled tin to plastic and the decoration changed too – but not the careful bustle involved in sandcastle building, the agreeable exertion of carrying water and feeling its weight in the bucket, sloshing it around a bit on the way. Children of successive generations have shared many of the same seaside experiences, the same games, the same set of contrasts between

dry and wet and light and shade but not the contrast
between crowded and deserted beaches. To children the
seaside used to mean great empty spaces in which to play
cops and robbers, war games, catch, tag, King of the
Castle, piggy in the middle. And the ice-lolly after lunch
when everyone huddled together under the sunshade, a
striped cloth anchored in the sand like half of a cabin. The
photographer would come by every now and then on those
flat Adriatic beaches – a lot of people were there and yet
not so many – and he had toys with him which he'd lend
to the kids, bewildering and distracting them for the time
it takes to shoot a black-and-white photo. Looking at those
snapshots again after all this time and seeing once more the
swanlike shape of some old water-wings one remembers a
kind of material with an unforgettable feel to it...and
mama's knitted swimming costume.

building blocks

Oblongs, cubes, little columns, the coloured fronts of nordic houses, the tower with a clock drawn on it. The pieces were light and made of wood. Only a few possible combinations.

Later there was Lego with the idea of bricks and joints. But first you learned how to balance one building block on top of another; and whole cities – not single buildings, never mind little details like doors and windows – came to mind. Cities where there was no one outside, no one crossing the road. Winter cities where children played at home and were sent to bed early; fathers were affectionate, seen on Sunday; mothers always out of breath, worried about their dressmakers and hair stylists, ground down with familial duties, part-time work, orders for the maid. Outside there was the fog and the snow and a wide river with a short name. In the fog the occasional bicycle lamp. And you longed for the summer. And you couldn't wait to grow up.

catapult

You need a target for this one and strong hands and determination and good powers of concentration. A game for playing in the countryside, where hens fly before the energetic feet of boys. Schoolbooks inveighed sternly against the catapult. Let's have a closer look: a forked stick and two strips of elastic, each knotted – at one end to the fork, at the other to an oval-shaped piece of rubber. You could see the nest to be destroyed by the projectile from a long way off, the swallow chicks sitting there with wide open beaks. But chicken-chasing, on the other hand, never became a tragic affair because the victims could certainly hold their own. They'd hop off angrily if a stone burrowed into their feathers, looking around squintily, clucking together like old ladies commiserating about an injury.

chemistry set

This flat rectangular cardboard box contained test tubes, glasses, tiny dishes, filters, litmus paper, little flasks and vials with basic chemicals which had really peculiar foreign-sounding names; sometimes there was a microscope too. And there was a little book that explained how to do experiments. You could make soap, change the colour of certain powders – as well as their names, produce crystals and cause little explosions. Above all you could make a wonderful kind of invisible ink. Letters drawn with it on a piece of paper would appear on the paper when you brought it close to a candle, one after the other, as the you slowly slid it by the flame. The sheet would darken and give off an almost-burning smell, the words take on an antiqued colour. Children felt like sorcerers rather than budding chemists. They could always see the magic in things, that mutable soul-life they never doubted the existence of.

coffee grinder

It was meant for grinding coffee. But it looked like something left behind by dwarves or a toy that had gone to the wrong address. What on Earth was it doing in the kitchen? Why was it being humiliated up there among the ranks of saucepans and other cooking utensils? Wasn't it really a fairy dwelling? The wondrous little hut of some gnome? Usually it's the toys that imitate grownups' gadgets but the coffee grinder is the only adult appliance that unabashedly imitates a toy. It can't be lumped in with the wind-up telephone or the charcoal-burning iron in some museum of curiosities and antiquities, because the whole design is a complete parody. If you look at it, it's shaped like the sort of chest or trunk a kid might draw: a cube with a sloped roof. The handle and crank on top that work the grinder look like a silly version of the common chimney pot. And that window in the bell tower where you put in the coffee beans? Which genius of an architect designed that? To say nothing of the drawer-shaped door with that knob like a clown's nose on it.

Then there was the way it was used. The grinder had to be practically hugged. The housekeeper would push it against her fat bosom, keeping it at a slight angle in her lap, between her belly and thighs, her arm would make a wide circle and her wrist daintily danced in time to the rotation of the handle hidden in her hand. The smell of coffee would suddenly twist through the air. This of course is all happening in the kitchen, heart of the house. Now and again, outside, a car would kick up a roar of acceleration along the Via Emilia. You wouldn't hear that today. It was the sound cars made when there were less of them and plenty of room on the roads. You could hear one coming from a long way off like a crescendo of galloping hooves. It would reach a peak in an instant then diminish just as quickly with the sad echo of a fading siren. And each time, that rapid swelling and subsiding of sound left a trace of longing – brief, but recurrent – joining the wave of sound outside each time a car braked to the wave of hope inside of that it might be your parents returning home.

I don't know if I'm right to include the coffee grinder in with the toys. I don't remember when it became a toy. But that's what happened at some point. It must have been long after the scene with the housekeeper because by then we'd lost all track of her. Today that coffee grinder, painted red – it was bare wood then yellow then light green – belongs to me, now a grownup, and another little child who's never seen coffee except ready-ground and doesn't know anything about its grinding function. He uses it as a cash till. He slips money into the little drawer and when the game's over leaves it upside-down and open. Then I take it from him and stow it high up on a kitchen shelf where, still permeated with the old aroma, it watches over us. What a talent wood has to absorb and preserve the past!

cuckoo clock

Technically speaking, the cuckoo clock belongs in another catalogue altogether – the one for clocks. But actually it's something that's got itself into the wrong category. Its real purpose isn't telling the time but being looked at. Looking and imagining is the game you play with the cuckoo clock. The clock is the mechanism that lets the little birdie show itself and sing out its desperate cry; it's far less vivid than the little prisoner inside it who's forced to wait for the hour and the half-hour. The clock face with its numerals, the hands of wrought metal are ornamental, just like the little paintings on the wooden house. The house is just too pretty to be true – and it's not. It's a trap for innocents, an enchanted dwelling of some Witch of the North. Perhaps, long ago, a humble Swiss artisan created the cuckoo clock to give to his children on Christmas Day. He hid a tiny cuckoo inside it, thinking of his little ones who'd peek behind the clock's door and cry out with pleasure to see the creature fly out. But a selfish fairy fell in love with this new invention and stole it. She chained the bird to stop it escaping, only permitting it to sing each time the little window of its captive nesting place was opened.

In those lucky homes that possessed a cuckoo clock, it was hung high up on a wall. It had long chains and weights in the shape of pine cones which cast fluctuating shadows on the wall. The actual pendulum was a carved wooden ivy leaf. It moved inexhaustibly back and forth, stirring its comforting regularity into the silent air. The little bird would appear and disappear with such speed that you could never really see it properly. A spring roughly shoved it in and out. You watched for it attentively, nose in the air, holding your breath, prepared to catch every nuance of the rhythmic cadence of its cry and of its comings and goings. Then the door would shut with a muffled click. There remained in the air the repeated echo of 'cuckoo, cuckoo' and the sad anxiety of having to wait until its next appearance. One dreamed of walls covered with clocks all telling different times so that you could see cuckoos pop out non-stop one after the other.

Whatever the children were doing they would always stop dead in their tracks when they heard the cuckoo so they could take a look at it. And its sound was all of a piece with the opening and shutting of the hatch, the hasty dash outside, the rapid throwing open of its beak. And every time you saw that wooden shutter close tightly in front of you, you'd experience feelings of sadness, of loss, of longing, of nostalgia. And every time, you'd always forget to count up the 'cuckoos', so you never knew what time it was.

darts

Mysterious numbers ran around the cork target with its yellow and blue or black and white sections and concentric circles. They were there for the scoring but no one knew the rules so the winner was whoever got nearest the centre. The darts were metal-tipped; dangerous. There were stories about little children getting one right in the eye and the consequent screaming, blood, and rushing down to the hospital. The very smallest children would shiver and were almost too scared even to touch them. These days the danger has gone. Now they're tipped with rubber suction cups or instead of darts you have ping-pong balls wound with velcro strips that stick to a fabric-covered board. But those games aren't the same. The great thing about real darts was weighing them between your thumb and forefinger before the throw. You would spin one, two or three times with your whole arm, keeping the wrist rigid, at shoulder height. Then the dart was launched. It would cleave the air like a rocket and halt at a perfect 90 degrees to the target. The slightest uncertainty in the throw would cause flight errors: the dart would clunk awkwardly against the wall and fall to the floor, robbing one's throw of all grace. It would seem to disintegrate, to go all floppy.

Once I happened to see some skinny boys in short pants with the flights of darts peeping out from their pockets. They were running amongst the trees throwing them at the tree trunks with an air of magnificent insouciance.

disks

They are a game, similar to bowls, played by children – especially at the seaside where burying them in the sand is an indispensable part of the fun. You can see children with their legs apart, up to their ankles in the sand exploring the cool moistness with their toes while they dawdle about waiting for their turn to throw. The disks don't sink but rest on the surface or half bury themselves into a dune. It sometimes happens that a disk thrown with particular enthusiasm falls on its edge and shows only a half moon shape. Then the issue becomes whether or not it's a valid throw. They come with a smaller disk which is thrown first. The disks are semi-rigid wheel-like things made from moulded rubber and have concentric ridges and a small hole in the middle. Once you have one in your hands it's absolutely impossible to resist the desire to bend it. You begin toying with it, sticking a finger through the hole and turning it around. Or you make a tower of disks under the beach umbrella. Or you hold up as many as you have between your hands and then let them rain down one by one. Or throw them like flat stones on water, counting how many rings they make, imagining flying saucers against the sun and vie with your mates to rescue them from the bottom of the sea. On floors by contrast, you try to get them to roll along, to revert to the original function of their prototype, the wheel. The Mayans invented the wheel solely for play purposes and every child reinvents it for the same reason. More than the game it's meant for, a plaything is usually remembered for its personal, incidental uses. And for its smell, its sound, its texture. A disk placed between the teeth will stimulate the appetite, a reminder perhaps of teething and the plastic rusks a mother would provide to soothe the pain.

diver

Now, instead of divers they have spacemen – astronauts wearing spacesuits and boots – who really look just like the old toy diver. He was a little blue or grey man enclosed in his diving suit with a little plastic tube for breathing. You filled the bath up to the brim and got him to walk along the bottom fishing for imaginary fish while you stayed outside. The other kids around you would clamour to take the strings from your hand; there were never enough divers to go around. It a was a rather unusual toy that no longer exists. Even the name is old-fashioned, now they say frogman or scuba diver.

There was an old drawing in the Children's Annual called 'The Diver in Love'; you could see the eponymous diver kneeling to a siren whose breasts were rather poorly concealed by the bra of her bikini. They were on the seabed amongst the fishes, and little bubbles of passion were escaping from his cumbersome diving suit. Her nakedness, his probable, albeit hidden, good looks, disturbed children in a way they didn't understand. They caught a mysterious glimmering of what the relationship between men and women must be like, an illumination of a secret part of the body that's vaguely sensed in the warm end of the belly, down there between the legs.

doll's house

That feeling of being Gulliver in the land of Lilliput. With the power to look into other peoples' houses and garner private moments of their lives for oneself. Rather like when a train slows down in a village, almost skimming the little houses, and you can look through the window and see a woman doing her housework, some old chap sitting around idly, or some young man still in his pyjamas yawning, unaware that anyone can see him. The doll's house wasn't really made for playing with but for close observation. It had two or three floors, an old-fashioned sloping roof, old parquet tiles riddled with woodworm, a front door and a French door at the back opening onto a perfect garden. On the ground floor, adjoining the hall, was a living room lit by three large windows; opposite that, a study, much smaller. Upstairs the bedrooms and the bathroom. Under the roof was the attic where there was an ironing room and a garret room for guests. Every room was perfectly furnished. There were walnut bookshelves in the library, brown leather ottomans, a piano in the sitting room, Tyrolean knickknacks in the kitchen and wardrobes with proper mirrors in all the bedrooms. The attention to detail! Wallpaper with a different pattern in each room, hand towels neatly folded and arranged in a chest of drawers, books piled on bedside tables, embroidered sheets, flowers in painted vases and fruit in a bowl on the break-fast-room table.

Voices would rise from the house and chase each other with the muffled echoes of fantasy from floor to floor and one would hear steps, slow or racing, going up and down the stairs. There were no dolls in the doll's house. Its inhabitants were imaginary beings whose presence was evoked and it was the objects that evoked their presence. The term 'Doll's House' shouldn't be taken too literally. The 'doll' alluded to is the little girl who owns the toy and who's supposed to study her future environment so she can learn how to do the difficult job of managing a large family. But actually the little girl is dreaming. She doesn't feel compelled by complicated things that involve lots of other people, she just likes to look and listen from her privileged giant's-eye-view. She lifts off the roof, a bit embarrassed by her power, and looks around, poking her fingers through the tiny windows, opens dressers which hide dinner services – ordinary ones and ones for special occasions, tidies up cushions on beds, folds down bedcovers, shifts upholstered chairs around, opens and closes trunks that someone's lined with paper, adjusts hangers (the old cross-shaped wooden kind) in wardrobes. All this activity isn't playing but the carrying out of an investigation. It's done with bated breath, almost as if the rightful owners might turn up, the ones who are just the size to live in such a house and would have a right to be upset. If it is a game then the game is in the riskiness of intruding and in the excitement of transgression. Of examining all the evidence and discovering the secrets of others peoples' lives. Those innocent secrets like family habits, mealtimes, the brand of toothpaste used, the chimes of the clock, the scent of the soap, the names of the medicines in the first aid cabinet.

The Dolls' House was handed down from mother to daughter. Like a photograph album it contained the family's story, bringing into the present some of the certainties of the past. Memories of slower rhythms and of things made to last were stored up in the solidity of its wood. But by the nineteen-fifties dolls' houses were being made out of plastic with components that could be taken apart; and the insubstantial pieces were bound to end up scattered around, here and there.

dolly

The dressmaker's place was always down at street level, or in a gloomy basement where you needed to put the light on even in the early afternoon. The atmosphere was unmistakable, a well-matured stuffiness, a musty blend of thread, fabric and breath. There was the kind of clutter – dressmakers' dummies, basted frocks, pincushions, scissors, irons, fashion magazines – that held no interest for the little kid made to go along with mother for endless fittings. The declaration 'Today we're going to the Dressmaker's.' was almost worse than that other woeful announcement 'We're going to the doctor's.' The day would start to look distinctly grey. Boredom, irritability and gloom would descend like clouds of rain.

The dressmaker was always exactly the same in whichever city and in whichever dressmakerly incarnation she happened to be found. She always wore some sort of castoff for a dress and drab woolly slippers with wedge heels. It was hard to tell her age although presumably she was quite youthful as she usually had young children. You divined the existence of these children, forever in another room somewhere, from their trail of broken and grubby toys and you'd hear long accounts of their caprices and their rascally doings from the mother herself. Rather tedious recitals, punctuated by the 'Oh, really?' of the distracted client. The worst thing though, wasn't having to sit through the endless hem-basting sessions hearing about 'pleats' and 'round-the-waist' while the customer slowly spun around as the Dressmaker knelt with pins in her mouth and spit on her lips. The worst thing of all wasn't even getting roped into the torment of measuring-up. ('Now let's measure up', the Dressmaker would say producing her ruler and her pen. And she would start to work out arm length, thigh length, how much round the waist, hips, bust, then carefully note down everything in one of her well-thumbed exercise books). Worst of all was the dolly.

She would sit in the middle of the double bed in the marital bedroom. Dressmakers' bedrooms all shared certain characteristics: feeble and dispiriting lighting, a little stand with a mirror – supposedly a 'dressing-table', a fake satin bedspread, worn-out bedside rugs and The Dolly. And the worst of the worst was that moment when the Dressmaker would ask her customer's little girl: 'Do you want to see the dolly?' then take her by the hand to the bedroom alcove. 'You can touch her', she'd grant with a smile. Her blonde curls were synthetic. Some versions had a bonnet held on with a large bow. Her dress was late eighteenth century in style. It was decorated with trims and lace and opened into a bell shape to conceal her stiff legs. Two titchy feet emerged from beneath her skirt, stuck into little white socks and shiny black shoes. The dreariness, the sheer ugliness, culminated in the handbag that she dangled from her little pink arm held doggedly aloft. One couldn't bear to look at her face for too long because of its ghastly complexion – celluloid got up as porcelain.

Certain little girls didn't actually succeed in playing with their dollies. One dolly called Marilyn – blonde with big blue eyes - got two fingers through her eye sockets one morning in 1956. The gaping black holes left in her charming little face made her seem much nicer and instead of chucking her out it was decided to keep her. But it wasn't ever on to play those mummy-and-daughter games with her. Even in her disfigured state she was still insufferably vain and conceited. The only pleasure to be had was in degrading her – shaking her and then listening at her belly to the noise of those azure eyes rattling around and around. A few years later her hair was cut off. Someone said 'It'll grow back.' It never did. And so ended the vain life of Marilyn, still holding her arms out with a simpering smile. Nobody made a fuss this time and the last memory of her that remains is of her elegant feet – one bare and the other encased in a white sock, with her shapely legs held straight and slightly parted, sticking out from amongst the artichoke stalks in the dustbin where she'd been plunged head first.

fort

At one time the fort was all of a piece and made of wood. A square courtyard with a sturdy tower at each corner. Every boy had one just as every girl had a doll. Inside the courtyard, depending on its size, were one or more stables, living quarters and, in the middle of the square, the American flag fluttering in the breeze. The soldiers would enter through an opening in the stockade and pass under an arch of horizontal beams supported by vertical logs on which was picked out in red the words 'Fort Apache' or 'Fort Texas' or something of the sort. The little soldiers were of solid plastic and dressed in brown and blue with kerchiefs around their necks and hats on their heads. They were called *i Cow-boys*. The Indians, with feathers around their foreheads, long hair, wide trousers, naked bronzed chests and axes in their hands were always *gli Apaches*. And they were the favourites. They had strong painted faces with furled lips. They made brave attacks on the fort, surprising the enemy, striking them down with their axes or lances and throwing them off the towers. At the end of the fight the Indian chief would arrive on his horse, tear down the flag and ride roughshod over it. The Yankees would always win the war – even a little kid knew that – but in play the Redskins would have the honour of winning the battle.

guns

It was unthinkable that a little girl should ask Father Christmas for a pistol or a rifle! She could play with guns that belonged to her brothers or their friends when they let her. On occasion the boys would fiddle around with dolls and the girls would do some shooting. Such exchanges did occur. You would enter the territory of the other conscious of your own incompetence or you would put on an air of boastful superiority. The boys tried to give the dolls their baths, drowning them amidst splashes and cries from the little mothers and then shaking them about upside down. The girls clumsily copied the grimace the little boys made when they shouted 'You're dead!', or leapt around waving pistols in the air or sat astride armchairs pretending to gallop and take aim at Indians. But they usually preferred to limit themselves to just studying this strange object, making the cylinder spin over and over again, fascinatedly repeating the click of the trigger so like the snapping of a terrier. They liked to warm up the wood or plastic butt in the palm of the hand and feel how the fingers fitted perfectly in the grooves provided to enhance one's grip. Rifles were another matter altogether, more a question of skill and having the eye for it; and here it was the grownups, no matter which sex, who came out on top. Target practice would be organized at home, just like at the funfair shooting range, there was a card with concentric circles, a green one, a white one and a red one with corresponding scores, 50, 75 and 100, drawn on the belly of a fierce-looking redskin. The gun was loaded up with darts and you set your sights on the big red dot with the lovely round number 100.

What took most effort was keeping the barrel steady while simultaneously squeezing the trigger with your finger. The tension rose as the others joined in, surrounding the one who was shooting and bawling out advice, correcting your aim, saying 'like this', 'no', 'more to the right', 'more to the left'. Often the match would end in a scuffle.

The girls were afraid of the explosions and the sulphurous smell made by certain special caps which were bought for a few *lira* at the tobacconist's, against parents' wishes, and that brothers loved to let off by their ears and between their feet when they came out of school. But they were crazy about the popgun which had a little bit of cork tied to a string, tied in its turn to the trigger guard. The cork stopped up the barrel. When you fired, the cork would jump out with a dry sound like the smack of a kiss.

But the guns that both boys and girls liked best were the guns that were forbidden because they were real. So strong was the parental ban on touching them that you still believed they were highly dangerous even when they were unloaded. They'd be well wrapped up in fabric cases like musical instruments and kept in a rack. Grandfather would weigh out the gunpowder on the kind of little balance with two pans which by that time could be found only in the chemist's shop. He would fill the cartridges, made from pasteboard set in a metal base, with the powder and then they would take their places in the round compartments of the belt and bandolier. Children were only allowed to touch the spent cartridges, which smelled of that burnt smell that only spent cartridges smell of. When the men went hunting they would leave at dawn and very rarely took any kids with them. And almost never the little girls because they get all upset and want to stop the slaughter of the brown woodcock and the plump quail. Out hunting was when the real rifle went into action. First it was opened and folded down, two cartridges dropped into the double barrel. It was shut with a clean action and a smooth clunk. Then the shot would be fired, unbearable, deafening. The kid who'd been allowed to have a go would excitedly hold the rifle with a grownup's help. The small finger squashed under the bigger adult one would get bruised and painful. The recoil would make you stagger back. At last the bulky and unrestrained adult body that had squeezed and crushed you in a tug of tangled hair, rolled up ears, and cheeks reddened by prickly beard hairs, would let go of your child's body. And like an animal tied up too long you'd run off to kick about a bit.

One went back to the toy guns with greater determination. Aware of their cruel nature one used them more thoughtfully. Meanwhile a parcel of dead birds would be casually tossed onto a table before the duly horrified womenfolk who were supposed to cook them up.

kaleidoscope

The tube's made of cardboard with a jolly pattern and feels warm to the touch. The slightest movement and you hear the shuffling of tiny hooves, or grains rolling around and around. You can't resist having a look inside – but it's exhausting, because keeping one eye open and the other eye squeezed shut while simultaneously rotating the cylinder with your fingers is not so easy for a little kid. The number of possible patterns isn't infinite; now and again, without rhyme or reason, the little pieces of coloured glass will arrange themselves into patterns the viewer has seen before and he will smile to himself, rather pleased to have spotted them again. One game involves the re-creation of specially selected patterns by attempting to goad the particles into one arrangement rather than another. Or you can just abandon everything to chance, limiting yourself to noticing a particular pattern whenever it crops up; or you can squint right down into the corners of the tube to find out where the reality of the mirrors begins and the illusion ends.

kite

It was a game for the autumn. We'd all go up the hill, grownups and little ones together. One of the grownups would be in charge of operations and hold the string, slackening it if it got too taut, pulling and winding it in if it went slack. Everybody chased after the strange bird that shook its ribbons and wriggled and writhed as it tackled the air currents. Its obvious instability made you anxiously hold your breath. And the disappointment (or satisfaction) came quickly enough, the kite came to grief almost straightaway, as if shot down by some unerring hunter. It wasn't very clear where the charm of this ethereal object came from. Perhaps from ancient rites, half-remembered as in a dream, in which kites represented the souls of the dead at the mercy of the wind, their wings pitilessly clipped, their bonds with the earth not yet quite severed.

There was one kite-owner who had made his kite with a meticulous attention to the prescribed proportions ('length should be to width as seven is to four') and wouldn't let the children touch it. But he drew them along like the Pied Piper of Hamelin. And that group of red-cheeked outcasts, their noses in the sky, followed the fine string high as the rain with their gaze, determined not to lose sight of the twisting diamond shape so burdened down with their fears. Tiny in the sky and huge on the ground when it lay in defeat on the grass, often the kite would come back from its flight broken. A wooden strut would be snapped off or the flimsy paper torn and sure enough the owner would declare the game over and his face would grow sullen as the kids' faces waxed incredulous. Such a lot of effort to get to the top of the hill, so much wind in the hair, through the trousers, up the skirt, and the hanging around and the failed attempts and the holding one's breath in for just a moment's flight so brief one hardly noticed it. The string and the coloured lozenge almost disappeared against the light so that we had to point them out to each other in order to find them. And then we'd lose them all over again. Grounded in the garage, its red paper torn, its tail rings come unstuck, the kite seemed like some other, gigantic object while it had seemed so small, so delicate against the clouds, and had been held to be as strong and unstoppable as a comet.

As the years passed, this thing, which had never been exactly jolly, got mixed up with a line from a very sad poem – 'happy is he that see only kites fall to the wind' – and forever enveloped in the stale odour of school desks, sweaty hands, erasers, chalks and playtime snacks. But with few regrets. Who complains about the disappearance of kites? Does anyone mourn them? Now that bodies themselves have learned to take flight, who attaches a string to aerial dreams?

lego

It wasn't that easy to recreate the models shown in the instruction leaflet. Real proficiency meant being able to make tall, structurally-complicated houses with balconies and roofs, separate entrances and stairways, without having a model to work from. Those little red bricks that fitted one on top of the other were capable of taking on infinitely extendable and quite surprising forms. If when you started off you didn't know quite where you were headed, you didn't need to work to rigid building specifications either. However, one's ability to assemble determined whether one would produce items to be admired or just have to look on with a sense of frustration. In the last analysis though, Lego is a game for the less-than-brilliant architect because he's not so beholden to his most exceptional creations. No one, except perhaps a jealous little boy, has the courage to dismantle a work that's required days and days to finish and which will be exhibited for weeks on end under the admiring gaze of guests. Once the builder has decided that it is time to destroy his creation, then he comes to know the bitter but somehow voluptuous pleasure of demolishing in a few minutes what has emerged only after a long painstaking process. He comes to realise the ultimate absurdity of all of our endeavours, the constant thwarting of our efforts that makes us rebuild and tear down and rebuild all over again. And every construction will be a mite different and become the starting point of new memories and longings, because you can never really do it exactly the same again. Even if Lego lends itself to the construction of a huge range of objects and can also be used to fashion animals and human beings and, now it's got more sophisticated, ships, aeroplanes, trains and spaceships, the shape for which it was invented in that long-ago, or maybe not so long-ago, year of 1937 is that of the house, the three dimensional realisation of a flat drawing on a sheet of paper. The solid rectangular house wherein dwells a child's idea of a family. It would be a fine thing to live in a red-and-green house of Lego with its tall windows, its gardens, roofs and chimney-pots.

little hercules, the
unknockdownable man

At some point commercials for Little Hercules started to appear on TV. He was a plastic puppet you blew up like a balloon, with a heavy weight in the base that kept him upright even if you punched him really hard. Hence the name, Little Hercules, The Unknockdownable Man. He had a silly grinning face, was a metre tall – maybe more, and had the innocent shape of a skittle. You got him by collecting tokens of a certain brand of cheeselets. It was the early seventies. For a few *lira* you could get these yellow plastic lemons with green screw tops from the grocer's that were filled with a very sweet synthetic lemonade which always left a weird plasticky aftertaste in your mouth. You could drink this stuff or chuck it away but it was really nice sticking your tongue in the opening or blowing into the empty lemon without putting your lips to it, so you could hear the air whistle and boom about, or take a look inside – screwing up an eye – at all that yellow. And you could get little thumb-sized bottles full of either tiny multi-coloured sugarballs or some syrupy liquid. And if you put a ten *lira* piece into the gum machine and turned the metal knob all the balls of gum got shaken around together and one would drop from behind the window with a 'plink'.

The little gifts you'd find in the cheeselet boxes had an excitement all their own; little square pictures that changed as you looked at them from different angles and flexible foam rubber stickers. If you collected enough points you could send off for a blow up Caroline the Cow in black and white with pink squeezy udders. Or Little Hercules himself. The reason he was so popular was that he was perpetually in motion which made him seem alive. The way he swung back and forth made him quite invincible in hand-to-hand combat. At last, here he was in the flesh – that secret friend, every child's invisible companion. The haves and the have-nots belonged to separate categories; Little Hercules owners constituted an elite society within the children's hierarchy, a special interest group.

marbles

The Beach. A kid is grabbed by the feet and dragged along so his behind makes a track. This is accompanied by a lot of laughing and squawking. Obstacles are built along the course; start and finish are outlined in the sand. Everybody chooses a marble and straightaway somebody doesn't like his or her colour. The red one causes the most arguments. The game almost always degenerates into a punch-up. The race is run amidst pushing and cursing and there's a good deal of cheating and generally unsporting behaviour. The grownups often have to intervene to sort out squabbles and separate parties engaging in hand-to-hand combat. I can't ever remember seeing a peaceful or harmonious game of marbles. The girls are all out in the first round and retreat almost relieved, because the great thing about marbles isn't the match but holding lots of them between your hands and listening to the music they make cracking against each other. And letting them slide from one palm to the other. Putting them in your mouth like cherries, rolling them against your cheek and shunting them around, carefully observing their serene displacements. Imprisoned in the glass are little helices of coloured plastic – yellow, azure or celestial blue, pink, green, red, and orange. Sometimes even two colours together. Little autumn leaves or flower petals mysteriously entrapped in a soap-bubble, tangled up in transparency itself.

On a sick child's bed marbles rolling around the coverlet create a universe of aquatic planets. The liquid material encloses the solid. Looking at light through one of these worlds the eye is overwhelmed by brilliance, seduced by the marble into a kind of self-induced hypnotic state where you learn the secret power of crystal balls. The name, like the thing it names, has strange magical qualities. Repeated over and over marble-arble-arble-arble-arble the tongue keeps its balance without rolling up or getting twisted. Children's play is spoiled by the surprising stability of marbles. One learns very young that the main thing about spheres isn't that they proceed in a straight yet circular motion, but that they possess equilibrium, perfection and fixity. If God exists, he is round like a marble.

matrioshka

Your uncle the Communist had been to Russia and come back a great enthusiast. Arguments would erupt, with fists thumped on the table and flushed faces. The men would stand up and glare at each other across the table under the lamp that cut the darkness with a shaft of light. The women would remonstrate all the while, demanding peace. The children thought Russia was nice. Uncle talked about it as a fairy land where everybody was kind and good-hearted. Of course those strange painted wooden dolls came from Russia – constructed from light birchwood, one inside the other, a refined version of Chinese boxes. The name alone was enough to paint a mental picture. 'I'll bring you a matrioshka' uncle had said on his departure. They made you think of a plump mama, good at baking cakes, kindly, dedicated to home and children. The complete opposite of real mothers: sophisticated, strict, irritable, tired.

And the matrioshka really did have such a calm face, so perfectly round with big sweet black eyes, which, like her cheeks – two pink dots – and a tiny red mouth, were drawn directly onto the wood. Her body, so broad and substantial, reminded you of an easter egg. She had an upper part and a lower part. She opened up and gave birth from her womb to a second, almost identical, doll and from that one came another and then another and so on until you got to the smallest one which was one solid piece. One doll was a variation on the next one with just a single detail different, the way a bow was knotted, the shade of a flower on her dress, the expression in an eye or a squiggly line on her kerchief. Put all together in a line or as a group they conjured up a cheery lineage of womenfolk. Womenfolk in waiting – waiting for a child to come, because all of them, except that last one, are rounded and could hide another doll inside themselves. Hide her from the masculine gaze perhaps – which would first admire her and then make her fruitful. A matrioshka's arms were full of tenderness; they indicated a naturally submissive disposition. And attached to her short arms were plump hands, with closed fingers, her palms held against an expectant belly. Drawn flat on the wood they wrapped around her body and guarded it, an upright body, as if she were standing to attention. Her large mild eyes told us how she floated in the beatific latitudes of her pregnancy, on the far horizon of the incommunicable secret.

Both boys and girls played with the matrioshka. The game was to take her apart and put her back together again a hundred times, working out the progression of shapes from the smallest to the biggest, making the design on the top section match perfectly with the one on the lower section. Even a little child could see that this Russian doll was something more than just a toy and so didn't object to her being kept on a side table or in the glass cabinet for precious things. Every home should have its matrioshka – or matrioshkas; household guardians, goddesses of the family hearth.

model cars

They were all carefully lined up in the window, each a precise copy of the original but in a concentrated miniature form. Created for collecting, model cars lent themselves to garage games, racing and staged accidents. But they hardly ever retained their original shiny chrome finish. Chucked any old how into a box in the kids' room they would have lost at least one wheel, a window, the bonnet, seats. What kind of a car is a car without wheels? And yet their little owners knew how to make them go anyway, fonder, one might think, of the little cars that were veterans of infinite battles on the dangerous highways of playtime, than the newly minted ones, so haughty because still so perfectly intact. There was a wind-up sort made of tin which had a little key on the side. You'd stop the wheels with one hand while the other turned the key - - hard work, tiring for the arm and wrist. But they made a lovely froggy sound which turned into the grating of the cicada when you put the little car on the ground to make it go. It took off quickly and then gradually slowed down till its noisy engine cut out, dying like an animal with a few spasmodic jerks.

A disturbing oddness of model cars (now they no longer have passengers' faces painted colourfully on the windows) was their unreal emptiness. The player would steer them from outside. He would poke a finger through a side window and turn the wheel while using his voice to imitate the sound of the engine. The door would open and an invisible phantom would get out. Modern versions made for the very young have introduced a nation of little toy-people who crowd inside cars which have been stripped down to the bare essentials to make room for them all. But with this, the game changes and becomes theatre. The race, the movement and the crash aren't important any more. No, the model car has to be empty to accomplish its task properly. It must provide comfort yet also independence, be enclosed and speedy.... Pure style.

music box

Here's a word (*Il Carillon*) that makes no mystery about what it means, the very sound of it is music. The ballerina with the white tutu awakes from her imprisonment inside the lacquered box. She dances on red velvet before the mirror set into the lid. The waltz is over, she comes to a halt. With her arm so gracefully arched, she waits at the ready, not knowing whether she should dance on or go back to sleep. Hair black as ebony, lips red as blood, her prince is the hand that turns the key to wind the mechanism. Merely opening the box isn't enough, the ballerina gets to her feet but just stands there, paralysed by the silence. Only the music can give her life. The melody drives her around and around in an infinite pirouette. A little click every three turns and she changes direction. Her loneliness is devastating.

She always came to mind at odd moments. In the lull between games when all other possibilities had been exhausted. Find the music box in the bedroom, wake up the princess. The gentle creak of the lid, she trembles like a butterfly. On demand she'll repeat her dance, compelled as she is by a melancholy enchantment. She is in love and awaits someone. Every time she hears the box open she thinks it must be her beloved. And she dances because it is ordained that she dance and the children, so peerless as an audience, never take their eyes off her.

The music box, this gleaming oblong of black wood, is always ready to spring to life, as all toys are wont to do at night. The inside is nut brown and lined with satin or velvet. It's divided into little compartments and has a false bottom – but there's nothing in it. Only the few notes of a refrain and the unvarying step of the dancer. (The same name is also used for a kind of musical toy for newborn and young babies that is made from plastic, fabric or tin. You work them by shaking them or by pulling on a string or turning a handle. They're just noise boxes really but they have a soothing effect.) Someone, though, got the idea of stripping the music box down to its bare mechanism, so now what you see in people's houses are little drums with pins sticking out of them that make metal strips vibrate at different pitches, thus creating the music.

And there you have the mysterious miniature orchestra that you imagined, as a child, to be hiding under the delicate feet of the little ballerina.

nails

The stem was an elongated oblong, with a hard plastic crown. They were three centimetres long and novel in design and construction. What you did was stick the coloured nails into a special perforated paper board to form simple mosaic designs: cottages, trees, geese, toads, flowers, ships. Those cleverest at this game would attempt to create faces. And sometimes you'd put the nails into your mouth to get a better appreciation of them. The tongue would pass over the rough shaft, meeting the pleasurable roundness of the head which would be licked to obtain the pretend-sweetness of the saliva produced by sucking on something. It was a toy that denoted seclusion; a toy for being alone or being ill. And just as you were going to sleep your feet might touch the surface of a nail that had got lost in the sheets between your feet. You'd clutch it between your big toe and your little toes without letting any of this show on the outside. Arms stayed nicely on the bedcover, eyes were kept closed, while the feet rolled the little thing around trying to get a long and enjoyable tickling and a smile would flutter on the lips, the rudiments of a giggle be held back down in the throat. Like this you could just drop off to sleep without holding a hand, without listening to a story.

pea-shooter

If children are told to treat someone with special care that someone falls under a cloud. Children make up a secret code to talk about him and he is watched constantly and suffers relentless attacks from the pea-shooter. Ambushes are organized and he's shot at from trees or windows when he passes by. The projectiles used to be pointed cartridges which the children would make for themselves...very dangerous things which could badly injure the eyes or enter the aural canal and damage the eardrum. Something like that occurred and the missiles got swopped for harmless little manufactured pellets, in white, red, yellow and blue, which would float off lightly into space. Most times they didn't hit their target but scattered about. They were made of compressed paper and were rather insubstantial. And yet they had a certain charm. One took aim quickly and blew hard down the celluloid tube. The torpedo was launched and you hid, hoping to get away with it, but exhilarated by the fear of discovery, you couldn't refrain from thrashing about clumsily and cackling madly.

pedal-car

Busily playing ring a ring o' roses, the girls barely managed to conceal how covetous they were of the pedal-car. The driver pushed down on the pedals with a glee quite out of proportion to the rather modest speed he could achieve and there was the most amazing clanking racket. Next to the steering wheel which he'd haphazardly spin around he had a manually-operated hooter, but he'd prefer to use his own voice and only pretend to push the horn. 'Beep-beep, beep-beep' he'd bellow. The car was a red open-top one-seater. The little girls always used to hope that its owner would get tired, get out and leave it unattended for a moment. But the wait was eternal, even worse than queuing for the swings. In the end they'd dispense with all pride and grovel for a ride. The boy would gloat victoriously and tread the pedals harder than ever. Sometimes he'd shout out, 'Later', and when he passed the girls he would be so besieged with protests and pleas, 'At least let us get in for a minute!', that it made him quite ecstatic. And he wouldn't stop.

Real cars were grey, brown or white, enclosed and oppressive. The Fiat Topolino had arms to hold the bonnet down, like those on a pram; the Lancia Ardea had a divided rear window that looked like a pair of glasses. The indicators stuck out of the body like thin rickety arms. The Fiat 600 was the car of the future, the up-to-the-minute model for the larger family. Buying a car, like buying a television set, was a social event. The neighbours would come round to see it and congratulate you. Test drives would be arranged with one's friends and kids were continually hoisted on and off somebody's angular knees. On the other hand, the pedal-car was never shared with anyone, it was an exclusively individual luxury.

Spring was the season for pedal-cars, along with bicycles and roller-skates. All through the winter you got up in the dark and went off to school in what still seemed to be night. In spring children swarmed in the streets, inundating the little paths along the riverbank and the games would be played in that clear clean light of good weather without scarves wrapped round your mouth and with your hands unfettered by any gloves. The pedal-car whizzed along, so you couldn't manage pedals really before you were four and even then one needed a brief apprenticeship to acquire the art of thrusting with alternate feet, something different to the circular push of the tricycle. When it was invented at the turn of the century the child's car had pedals and a chain just like a bicycle. But kids didn't like this cross-breeding and the toy went on to acquire pedals which were attached to a rod concealed under the bonnet. This arrangement made for a far better imitation of brake and throttle.

piano

A grand piano of course, black wood with three little removable feet. One screwed these feet, which looked like shrunken skittles, back on before beginning the concert. The fingers ran across the keyboard with exaggerated animation. The loose keys, not connected to anything, didn't put up the slightest resistance, begged to be mistreated. You just couldn't take them seriously; all they produced – a child couldn't kid himself – was a racket, a metallic tinkling, not music. Still you had the idea in your head; here is the great musician playing before a huge audience. Music though, belonged in the realm of the sitting room, to that other piano which was as full of beauty as the Madonna was full of prayer. One said one's evening prayers in bed; Grandma would sit by you and you would make the sign of the cross together. Then she would start the litany: glory to the Father, the Son and the Holy Ghost.... And the child would follow her trying to imitate the sing-song tone of her voice: as it was in the beginning so it shall be for ever and ever. And then together: Amen. And one went to sleep buoyant, with a feeling one could fly and with a happiness that captured the heart, and such joy it was almost melancholy.

picture cards

The card album never ever got completely filled. It would be put aside at some point while you started a new one. 'The Great Explorers', 'Wild Animals', 'The Charge of the 101st' and all the usual fairy stories. You'd buy three packets of picture cards after school with your weekly pocket money. Then you'd be off to a friend's house to swap your doubles while you waited for lunch, scissors and glue close at hand. Some hard-to-find cards had a value of up to ten. That's to say you'd only swap them in exchange for ten others. Even so you never managed to complete an album. Sometimes a double would be bartered for toys or tasks of a humiliating nature, like carrying a school friend's satchel all the way home from school or pulling down your knickers to be given an imaginary injection.

Card albums, like books, were invented for reading. (The picture captions explained things and were educational. When a card was missing it doubled the frustration because you were left looking at that empty space, the rectangular outline of the absent image, and reading the caption didn't make any sense.) But albums were also for writing in. At random. First there'd be a chapter or a sentence which would fit into the complete pattern afterwards. And the spaces left over were unresolved parts of a story which existed in full, somewhere; that had to understood and be put back together somehow. The album is satisfying because one creates with it. There is no album quite like another in the way it's assembled because, given the randomness of the little packets of cards bought by different children, the probability of the same succession of pictures occurring is like that of two writers writing the same book with the same words combined in exactly the same way.

But with footballer or cyclist cards you didn't make albums. They looked like portraits of the dead, like sad little saints. The star would be smiling in a pose that made him look as though he was holding his breath, his hair well brilliantined, the team shirt stretched across his swollen muscles, his name and a number written underneath. The boys would get quite excited reading these names and repeat them loudly to each other. And when they played with the cards they'd make so much noise you'd think there was going to be a fight. They'd blow on their card before throwing it. The experts at this game knew how to hold a card between the index and middle finger so as to throw it in a straight trajectory with a flick of the wrist. You won by getting your card on top of another and the more you covered the more you won. Or they'd play 'Wallcards'; they'd prop target cards up against a wall and then throw other ones, aiming to hit the target cards. Perhaps because they were such disorderly games, amongst the most tumultuous despite all the concentration they required, they flourished out of doors, usually along the pavement against the walls of houses and in the court-yards where from open windows you'd hear the amplified voices of women busy with their cleaning, sometimes singing or calling or bawling instructions about the housework: 'Turn off the gas', 'Bring me the carpet-beater' and 'It's time to lay the table'. The mothers who had housekeepers would, even when at home themselves, follow them around the house telling them what to do.

The lads would come in starving, sweaty and rumpled. They'd chuck cards down onto polished floors and newly-beaten sofas. They'd hold crumpled cards in their damp fists, crushing them as they stuffed them into the bulging pockets of their short trousers.

pick-up-sticks

Muscles tensed, jaw tightened, breath held in, that's how a small child plays Pick-Up-Sticks. The little sticks are enemy warriors to be captured. The finger pushes down on the end of one stick to raise up the end of another and take it away from the rival army without moving any stick but the one you want to seize. The initial pleasure is being first to play and grabbing all the warriors who are easy to get at and scattering them far from their unit. Then there's the ballet of push down and rise up, making one Pick-Up-Stick jump using the other Pick-Up-Stick without disturbing the whole pattern. Otherwise there's the disaster of the stick that falls back onto its unit and causes a collapse, with sticks rolling around to the other player's advantage. This means defeat. The enemy, sensitive to the tiniest tremor and capable of distinguishing the most infinitesimal vibration, will be jubilant. (That hateful phrase 'you've moved it' isn't even said out loud.) His booty will be lavish and plundered from you with impudent and vainglorious asides. The gravity of Pick-Up-Sticks is quite contrary to the good humour of tiddly-winks. Tiddly-winks is lively and disorderly. Losing doesn't seem so bad. You make a piece fly without getting tense about it, flicking it while spread out on the floor and shouting a bit. In Pick-Up-Sticks, in those critical moments when there's no easy stick, the requirement is absolute silence; a stern concentration that doesn't come naturally in childhood.

picture cubes

Four by four – with sixteen cubes you could make six scenes from fairy tales. A simple puzzle game, the sort of thing for afternoons on your own or when you were ill: the times when there wasn't even the shadow of a brother around and as a high fever got higher, the ogre from 'Puss-in-Boots' would turn into a mouse and Puss would eat it at least three hundred times and every time your feverish brain would imagine the agony of being eaten alive. Oh, never mind that it was a wicked ogre and deserved it. What if you reminded yourself of all the animals in the world that end up crunched between the teeth of a bigger animal, and you felt all alone and abandoned and thought that the window might open and let in a demon? What if suddenly, indecipherable letters appeared on the wardrobe and your hand searched hopelessly for something to take your mind off it like sorting out the pieces for 'Cinderella at the Ball' and every ghastly thing in the whole world, real or unreal, insinuated itself into the silence of your room? What if then you saw the face of the witch from Snow White who offered the apple in the face of an unmentionable person who was going to come into the room with some 'medicine' and poison you? What if you were a worm that crawled and you got chopped in two by a spade, or an ant that got squashed underfoot, or a zebra who was going to get chased and impaled on the fangs of some beast, or a fish and they hooked you or a lobster and they boiled you? Then what if you escaped by turning yourself into a whale, the biggest of them all, or a lion, King of the Jungle? But if they caught you they'd skin you to hang you up in the lounge or make you into a bedside mat and cut you into slices. And if you managed to become human, like Pinocchio did, then there would be whole new world of suffering and death ahead of you.

These fevered thoughts had two different effects during convalescence. Some children took to cutting lizards' tails off, setting cats on fire or throwing stones at sparrows. Others went around extremely careful about where they put their feet so as not to crush the ants, and would throw open windows to let the flies out before anybody swatted them.

pinball

A gang of kids, boys and girls, queue up in a bar for their turn on an occupied machine which busily chings away. If the player they're waiting for is a man he wears a rather serious expression, maybe even a scowl. His manner betrays no signs of triumph or jubilation. He concentrates on the ball, calmly depressing the buttons connected to the sprung flippers which whack it around. And the ball whizzes up and down the whole length of the sloped table, lighting lights, sounding bells, disappearing down the hole. The man drops coins in one after the other, completely ignoring the children. He pulls the release handle back then lets it go with a sharp snap to fling the ball onto the table. A cigarette trapped between his lips, an eye closed to shield it from the smoke, when he's not happy with his score he emits the barely audible hiss of a cautious snake.

The bar was always noisy and warm: outside grey autumnal skies, bicycles lined up in the rack; inside worn-out grey tiles on the floor, everything swimming in greasy yellow electric light. This is the workers' club where the men would talk about politics or soccer. The noise would be augmented by the clicking of billiard balls in the next room. An old man would sit motionless on a chair of woven plastic raffia. Every now and again someone would speak to him and he'd answer with clipped sure sentences. Coffee and glasses of wine were carried about. There were no women, only some little girls.

And a little girl playing pinball was a disaster. Often the boys would count her out, shoving her away from the machine. They'd really fret when a more determined creature would manage to take over the flippers, drop in her money and shoot off a ball. More out of spite than desire, because she couldn't actually see the point of this game men and boys would fight to play. The ball would slide around unmanageably, hitting obstacles and playing a sweet little tune on electric chimes. Numbers spun and stars lit up for the very best players, the ones who managed to keep the ball in play for a long time, and so didn't give up their positions; the ones who were deft enough to jostle the machine's sides with little shoves thus changing the ball's course. However in the end the ball would always shoot into the mouth of the central tunnel and run straight down, immune to any outside influence, to the dark abyss where it would be swallowed up with a metallic gurgle. You could hear the ball's muffled movements inside the machine as it made it's perpendicular descent, rolling to a final halt against the other balls. The spectators fluttering about the machine were divided in their allegiances. The bar's close fug embraced both those for the player and against the ball and those with the ball and against the player and there was noise and chatter and the tinkling of glasses and everything was wrapped up in an aimless mass of floating blue smoke.

plasticine

Before there was Plasticine there was clay softened with water. You'd knead it, pat it with your palm, cut it up and divide it into meatballs. Your hands would get dirty, your nails would get dirty, even your arms would get dirty. Plasticine is the clean version of this squishing game. The first stage is getting from the hardness of the block you take out of the cellophane to the pliability that comes with a lot of pulling, rolling and squeezing. This is when, with the substance in a docile state between your fingers, the first of your creations comes to life. You become like the Original Being alone in a universe still in its primeval state; you get bored and indulge the urge to create playthings out of unformed matter: balls representing the Sun, the Earth, the Moon, baubles for stars and a myriad of shapes for every earthly thing. The first shape that Plasticine lends itself to is the sphere, then from roundness one progresses to the cube and then to the cylinder. Pushing an open hand down onto a block of Plasticine one gets a pancake inscribed with a palm print; a lifeline, a line of fate, a heart line – a whole intricate network of lines that hold the secrets of future encounters, passions, illnesses…one can almost see there the deceiving knot of existence itself.

Plasticine has a smell children love which sets it apart from newer materials that do the same job of allowing form to be given to the formless. They are natural doughs that are harmless if swallowed but if they go floury they easily get brittle. Moreover, they don't resist with that initial stiffness that gradually succumbs to the relentless action of the fingers. When kneaded, Plasticine responds with a malleability and a special warmth. Because of this, many children secrete little balls of the stuff in the bottom of their pockets so they can bury restless fingers in it when they need to amuse themselves, improve their concentration or just calm themselves down.

pots and pans

In the days when radios were large pieces of furniture with knobs of rounded ivory, and record players were called gramophones and records weighed a lot and were easy to break, and irons were made of cast iron and were flat or tall like ships and you put glowing coals inside them. When some people still used those clumsy great steel stoves to cook on, the ones that you had to start a fire in, and a sturdy grey metal ladle hung from the ledge above the oven and the metal pasta colander had three long feet and little star shaped holes and the tub – light and tinny-sounding when struck – where the little ones had their bath was made of metal, and the sinks in the kitchen were enormous hulks made of marble and the sewing machine had its own handsome cabinet and a broad pedal set in wrought iron and a curved wooden cover with a handle on top. When television was something everyone watched together like the cinema and women wore stockings that needed darning. In those days children would receive as presents miniature sets of pots and pans and dolls' tea sets.

There were little copper saucepans, perfect copies of the big ones hanging in the kitchen with various shapes suited to their different uses, all with corresponding names; the cauldron that looked like a pail, the elongated fish-kettle for the fish, the milk pan for warming milk, the casserole with its lid and two handles on the sides, the frying pan for frying, the baking pan for the oven. The food was little stones, broken bits of other toys and leaves. Especially coveted were the leaf tips of rubber plants which, tall and shining, added a little splendour to the entrances of middle-class apartments and were the pride and joy of their owners. What might happen to these plants deprived of their tips, which were going to be fried up in little pans, wasn't a problem that interested kids, who were quite ready to put up with domestic fury for the sake of this splendid dish, to dismiss the rage of the parent in question and perform the same excision on another rubber plant.

The fine solidity of the little copper pots and pans was more than matched by the unthinkable opulence of the tiny blue and white porcelain tea service. The little round cups opened out into the most pleasing hollow shape that could be made. They were half the size of 'real' coffee cups. But what would a little lady do with such a fine tea set in the days when four o'clock tea was a peculiar phenomenon found only in English literature? She jealously guarded her little cups, kept them empty for fear of breaking them, watched them twirl around her finger, fell completely in love with them. That cup shape would mould itself onto other passions, returning in other incarnations, outlining desires apparently quite other in nature. It would crop up in the tastes and innocent obsessions of the adult woman, as in the phrase 'a storm in a teacup' which now sums up the truth of existence itself for her. The fierce concentration and carnal passion with which one loves things when one is small....

printing set

You couldn't believe your own eyes. Butterflies, dwarves, flowers, cherries: all appeared on the paper within precise ink borders. All you had to do was press the stamp into its blue-soaked pad and then press down again onto the paper. And if you hadn't pressed it hard enough you'd try to re-impress it; again and again and again and the image would distort into a dislocated vision, multifold, as if in motion....

puppet show

'If one could but read the furrowed brow and know the anguish that lies within those that one doth envy, rather one would take pity upon them'. 'And the lovers tryst like Arabia Phoenix, of which many may speak but none do know'. Grandma would recite these lines with a sigh, lines which rang out like proverbs to a child's ears. She would produce them whenever she presented a play for her little audience of grandchildren. The unsightly rather grubby puppets made of stiff plaster and dressed in faded material, which had been thrown into some corner, seemed almost to come to life. Grandma would jiggle them around from the top of a papier-mâché theatre. Mingling fairy tale with melodrama she'd make up stories of secret loves which always ended in tragedy. Here and there in the dialogue would pop up those arcane and magical phrases which grabbed your attention to such an extent that you hardly wanted anything else from the play except the marvellous moments when they would be pronounced. One dreamt to oneself of a beautiful creature like a peacock or a bird of paradise that could give form to unheard-of words like 'Arabia Phoenix' and 'the lovers' tryst'. One mulled over 'the anguish that lies within' and saw one's own private agonies so clearly portrayed by that puppet with the crumbling eyes crying out up there on the stage. You couldn't follow the story too well, you never knew which character was speaking. They all had Granny's voice. But it didn't matter as long as you could hear once again, holding your breath for a moment, that enchanted phrase.

Rag Doll

Little Miss Rag Doll is tender and witty, a chubby tomboy with a potato nose and zippy little eyes. With her toddler's clumsiness, here at last is a doll that personifies early childhood after a century of the doll as a mirror of elegance and adult femininity. She originated in the thirties, then became very popular in the fifties when children were beginning to be granted some liberty to choose things for themselves. The cloth is warm and rough, hands love to touch it for it arouses feelings of tenderness and affection. The Rag Doll has a fabric face and body, cloth dress and cloth shoes made in a child's style. She's got a short skirt that lets you see her legs, chubby and shapeless like a toddler's. Her hair isn't curly but straight with a squared-off fringe that reaches just to her ears. When a little girl hugs her she feels the warmth of a living body against hers; as she runs along hugging her, Miss Rag Doll's arms and legs gently flop about as if she wants to be put down.

rocking horse

Was it in Herman's on 42nd Street or at Lord & Taylor's or Saks Fifth Avenue? There was a full-size rocking horse in the entrance, with leather saddle and reins, all ready to be mounted. Galloping away on its curved metal frame was a wooden imitation – perfect in form and colour – of the common bay Arab horse. The children looked at it admiringly, the adults uncomfortably – how on earth could one resist the temptation to get up on it? It was pure torture. Since when were adults ever offered the chance to relive childhood sensations with gigantic grownup-size toys? At some amusement park for infantile regression perhaps?

On merry-go-rounds the horses were the favourite mount. Lined up two by two they galloped around in an undulating circle. The smooth hollow of the saddle affectionately accepted one's buttocks and the maternal swell of the belly opened out your thighs into a daring position. One felt the coolness of the pâpier-maché against one's skin. Perhaps they were right when they used to feel it wasn't proper for a woman to ride a horse with her legs apart: they'd divined the secret pleasure, the unavoidably delicious rubbing. A little girl riding her rocking horse is quite happy just with the motion, the thrusting alone, she doesn't need, as a boy does, to brandish a sword or call imaginary comrades on to battle. She rides in thrall to an innocent eroticism. Closing her eyes, letting the wind ruffle her hair she squeezes her knees together and, tensing her muscles, provokes a growing current of shuddering thrills inside herself.

That horse in New York was a giant version of the modest rocking horse found under the tree one Christmas. A disappointing present for children used to getting up on the golden palfreys of the merry-go-round. Skinny and squat, it didn't give off any sexual shocks. You needed to give it a damn good spurring to have any fun, to produce at the very least a make-believe gallop, but in the meantime one acquired that rich vocabulary of all things equine: hocks and withers, croup and fetlocks, horsehair and mane, pastern and hooves. It must have been its inadequacy compared to the original, with its mythical status, that determined the fate of the rocking horse. If, for example, the doll has evolved hand-in-hand with social and technological changes, then all the whimsical variations on the little horse must reflect some restless, unsatisfied search – some dilemma. They tried covering it with hair and even replacing it with another animal altogether, for instance an elephant or a bear. In choosing the rocker as the toy's main source of interest, they arrived at the idea of dispensing with the animal resemblance and stylizing the form. And in some cases the head is just suggested by a flat bar. There's one such kind made in Germany from pale wood which has a hole running right through the wood instead of eyes. Another horizontal board with rounded edges makes the rump. Long fair bristles serve as mane and tail, a simple cord as bridle. More a piece of decor than a toy, more an old nag than a noble steed. But never mind, still a step up from the broomstick. So often, in the world of toys, one regresses....

roller skates

In summer the iceman would go round the streets with his push-cart. He'd sell off his frozen blocks wrapped in sackcloth, nimbly ferrying them to his customers' houses. They went to feed the iceboxes, things that looked like the kind of freezers they have nowadays in bars for storing ice cream. You'd make bets on how long it would take for one of these clear oblongs from the cart to melt. It was a game without winners or losers – you'd bet just for the sake of it, because there was no way of finding out and adults, if asked, gave vague replies.

If you were going to go out roller skating, first you'd stop to have a look at the giant ice cube and absorb its freshness before working up a sweat. Holding yourself steady, grasping on to something for support, you'd try putting a foot out first in front and then behind, for the thrill of sensing the imminent tumble with the soles of your feet. Getting up on a pair of skates for the first time; this was a feat that required a bigger dose of courage than learning how to ride a bike. That's because you tend to master the bike bit by bit while with skates it's all done in one go; you slip them on abruptly one day, without any preparation, goaded and mocked by some older friend so you can't get out of it. You start off holding onto his hand, your free arm flapping in the air and swaying precariously at the knees. The ground becomes an impossible surface scattered with unmanageable little balls, you despair of ever succeeding and squeal that you want to stop. Then all of a sudden you harden your resolve, take the plunge and sail off on your own letting your feet do their job, and you feel the joy of the whole thing colouring your face, your breath whooshing in, your lungs filling up....

Excellence at skating was something acquired gradually and further refined with each bit of practice, shown off at first with pert superiority, later with the grace of a perfectly mastered skill displayed with little regard for the public eye. Skates then became an extension of one's body, a natural appendage, a means of locomotion through the complex adult world. But adults didn't like skates, they got irritated with all the racket they made under their windows, all that busy to-ing and fro-ing in front of their shops, by their open doors. You really race around the town on skates and a wide pavement would sometimes be selected for speed trials. More than by the spinning of skate wheels, the peace was shattered by all the squawking, arguing and raucous one-upmanship. In the summer kids of all ages used to travel in gangs, live in the streets, develop new, rascally personalities. They'd see themselves as belonging to the Foreign Legion, or as explorers from another planet existing temporarily in space. They'd subvert the grownups' peace and quiet; they were silence wreckers in perpetual motion. Alongside the random beat of squeals, cries and calls, there would be sudden collective increases in volume: explosions of shock, disappointment, anger or glee, the counterpoint of their voices becoming the predominant note in the air, leaping up from courtyards and coming in through windows like a song.

scoobeedoo

They overran the early seventies like a virus, a new epidemic. Playthings that rained down on children from an adult culture that was rejuvenating itself with the passion to wiggle oneself stupid again. Teenage boys and girls would gyrate their flanks inside large plastic rings with the americo-hawaiian name of hula-hoop (the *hula hula* is a dance from Hawaii); children had their own smaller version which could easily revert to its former function: to be rolled on the ground, pushed with a hand or a little stick as its owner chased along after it. Or you could make up gym exercises by raising the hoop over your head and jumping through it like a skipping rope. They were light, smooth inside and roughened on the outside where ridge-lines went around the circumference. In Paris the eighteen-year-olds dressed them up in pink or sky blue velvet for Christmas. In courtyards, gardens, even on landings, you could see adolescents practising away with hula-hoops around their waists, hips shaking in a Polynesian Tamurè dance, the hoop lagging a little as it spun around, then catching up and then sloughing off its rotations as it wrapped round the legs, rippling down to the feet. It was the time when the rapid beat of rock'n'roll poured from every radio and the air was filled with excitement wherever young lads played around in the streets. Meanwhile their pockets were stuffed with scoobeedoos.

These were thickly knotted ropes made up of interwoven coloured plastic strings, you could use them as key rings or just as lucky charms. Being able to make one of these was more a question of patience than skill. A few people could do it and they'd give scoobeedoos as presents to their friends. It was also fascinating to witness one being created as someone dexterously wove complex figures with the plastic strings, using the thumb to hold one still while the others were knotted together.

And how did little kids play with scoobeedoos? They'd twist and turn them between their fingers, while biting and gnawing one end with their teeth, allowing the plastic softness to rub up against their gums with increasing enjoyment. They were after the same pleasure that cats get when they gnaw away at telephone wires and throw back their heads and riffle their whiskers.

scooter

Wobbliness. Toes poised nervously on the footboard while the hands grip the handlebars. The other leg's supposed to push you along but it won't do it. It's trembling, curling up, stumbling. The slower you go the less you succeed. You have to give in to uncertainty, accept the risk and abandon yourself to a dubious stability. After that first moment of extreme courage all fear seems absurd and that dragging leg becomes as light as air and your body becomes at one with the thrust of pure speed. In Scandinavian airports they provide big scooters for the passengers, and agile grownups of all ages lightly scoot up and down the corridors, pushing the two wheels along rhythmically with serious expressions identical to those of the pedestrians they pass. What would a toy be like in these cold regions? Perhaps children who have to spend long winters at home try desperately to embrace the sunshine and throw themselves recklessly, impetuously, into the open air along those level streets of the North, deserted on sundays except for trams, bicycles and scooters. The scooter, these days replaced by the skateboard, both encourages and restricts heedlessness, wisely providing a choice of places for support: the ground and the handlebars. It's not a matter of acrobatics but of independence. It's nice to look at too with its geometric simplicity and basic functionality. Even if you never get up the nerve to have a go on it.

shuttlecock

The little conical basket would be gripped between your thumb and fingers, wide end up. With your index and middle fingers you'd depress a button that operated a small metal tongue inside the toy. The little tongue would retract then release giving the ball the velocity required to leap from its basket towards the basket of another player who was meant to catch it. The ball wasn't exactly a ball. It was a shuttlecock – half a rubber ball with a crown of plastic feathers set into the sawn off bit. It made you think of the head of a Red Indian and when it wasn't in use it would be sucked on with great satisfaction or gnawed at until the imitation feathers lost their proper shape and turned into formless blobs of saliva and plastic. The little basket had an attraction all its own – the noise its metallic tongue made as it bent, cracked and shot, you could disarm an adversary with this by working the mechanism just below his ear.

The word for Shuttlecock in Italian *volano* is similar to the verb to fly *volare* and there was another object, also capable of take off and flight, with the same name. It was a sort of collapsible wheel with five spokes. Threaded on a central pivot, it waved like a large flower supported by a stalk held in the hand. On this stalk was a ratchet with toothed gears. If you pulled hard on the ratchet, the gears would crank up, the pivot turn and the hoop would spin off into the sky just like a flying saucer. You'd play with it out in the open, following the hoop with your eyes, watching through the aperture made by your hands and squinting at the light, then run off to retrieve it from wherever it was hiding – the more inaccessible the better. It must have been sold under the name Flying Saucer in the shops. But the children preferred to call it *volano*.

skipping-rope

The rope's about two metres long. The handles should be made of moulded wood if they are to be enjoyable to hold. The tapered ninepin shape of the ideal handle fits perfectly into the palm and the wood's smooth porousness absorbs perspiration while maintaining an even temperature. If the rope's too long you twist it around the base of the fingers, shortening it to a suitable length. Skipping is a rotating movement; one draws an imaginary circle in the air with the rope, which then goes over one's head and under one's feet. It's all a question of synchronicity; you have to jump when the rope's down low, almost scraping the earth, but you musn't let it touch the ground. The more turns you manage without tripping up, the better you are at it. You can skip standing still, walk-and-skip or run-and-skip. And two can skip together, face to face, breath to breath. Or three can play. Two players face each other about a metre and a half apart. Each holds up one end of the rope. They let it go slack and begin to make it turn, this time its rotation imprints an ellipse in the air. Another player enters the ellipse; she has to jump over the rope every time it's about to catch her legs. When she trips – it always happens on the first pass or because the rotation speeds up – she has to give up her place, definitely the best one to have, to one of the other players.

Skipping with a rope, especially on your own, develops cheerfulness and self-confidence. Provided of course that you manage to get up to over one hundred. Otherwise you might as well give up.

One notices a feminine preference for this game. It must have something to do with the fact that a little girl's plaits twirl around with the rope, brushing the air and lashing her cheeks to her great pleasure. If you've never had long hair you can't imagine what a lovely feeling it is to feel it fly up and then slap back down on your shoulders.

skittles

The skittle has one of the most familiar of all shapes. It reminds you of a baby's feeding bottle. Crawling around the house on all fours, an infant discovers giant upside-down skittles in the legs of chairs and tables. Making skittles tumble by substituting yourself for the ball, then listening to the angry shouts of the players, was remarkable if incomprehensible fun. Depositing yourself in the midst of the fallen skittles and refusing to move, holding on to one and crying if they tried to deprive you of it thus forcing your brothers to call your parents, then being picked up and sweetly cajoled; all this was the wonderful world of the skittle, as mysterious as its clatter of a name.

soap bubbles

To make soap bubbles you needed your sleeves rolled up to your elbows, drinking straws purloined from the bar and some soap flakes. It didn't always work and even if it did it would result in a slippery mess in the kitchen or the bathroom and recriminations from mother. We would fill glasses with soapy water from the sink and take them to the garden, where we were allowed to play with bubbles. The straw was split four ways at the end (the dipping-in end). Now and again you had to give the liquid in the glass a shake and swell the foam by blowing into the water, then you puffed lightly and finally, out spat the wonderful transparent globe. If there were no straws you could try to make a ring with your thumb and forefinger, wetting them well, and then steadily, gently, blow a bubble between them. The height of proficiency was to produce a large sphere that could take off and fly without exploding – at least until it came to rest, and then, 'plop', it would disappear. However, the more usual convoy of little and medium sized bubbles, travelling with a slight drag through the air, was quite satisfying from an aesthetic point of view. They almost all tried to land on the ground where they would die straight away or on a leaf where they would last just long enough to refract all the colours of the rainbow. Sometimes one would finish up on your skin, breaking with a false sensation of coolness. Your mouth caught the bitter taste of soap, your eyes pure enchantment and your mind a disturbing realisation of insubstantiality. Sometimes in really cold weather a crystal would form inside the bubble, transforming it into a fairy grotto with miniature stalactites, where you might expect to spy the figure of an elf.

Nowadays you can buy ready-made plastic containers with bubbles; all you need to do is shake and blow through the plastic hoop. This way even a little child of three or four years old can play with bubbles, leapfrogging the whole preparatory stage. But being able to make for yourself a fabulous yet cheap toy (the cheapness of a toy increased its value in certain cases) was a sign of superiority in the hierarchy of childhood values. It established a distance between you and your peers and highlighted the distinction between being a small child and just a tiny tot.

soldiers

The Indians would take aim with a spear or a bow, balancing with their legs akimbo as if dancing or they'd shake their tomahawks above their heads with their knees raised or they'd stretch forward riding at a furious gallop, rifle in the air or with a shield for protection, or they'd squat down as they beat the drum. The cowboys had rifles and pistols, knee-length boots, wide-brimmed hats, horses ready at the trot. Sometimes they'd race along with a leg thrown out behind them, the other foot fixed to the oval-shaped base that stood in for the green prairie, but usually they were set in stiff postures and at most they would throw a lasso. The war between the cowboys and the Indians was the one most heartily felt. Adversaries were clearly differentiated and you could understand the reasons for their enmity at a glance. The Redskins, with their rituals around the fire, their wigwams, their deep sense of honour, respect for friendship, wise old men, silent womenfolk, belong to the world of childhood, to a version of the human race that suited a child's point of view. It was as if their defeat was written down as part of a child's destiny, the destiny of changing and growing up, of throwing away the face paint and the fancy dress.

Battles between the well-organized cowboys and the hot-headed Indians were always skirmishes. These fighting men never clashed in open country but spread out in the woods and set ambushes and traps for each other.

You could also play with the European toy soldiers; the French troops all in blue, Garibaldi's men in their red shirts, the English with gold braid on their chests, the Hussars with their tall plumes. You drew the armies up opposite each other and then you advanced your troops until they met in a total scrimmage.

Today's warriors are intergalactic travellers. It's not the past being imitated but a projection into a warlike future. As always it's the struggle of Good against Evil, now in the shape of defenders or enemies of the Universe. Children have instinctively grasped that the offensive is no longer limited to a particular territory but extends to the whole planet. The old style toy soldiers don't make any sense and have been done away with forever by super-beings and extraterrestrial supermonsters, exogenous creatures of fantastic shape which have necessitated the coining of new names. The 'sky-born' make war in the air. The children hold them between their fingers making them fight at eye level. Battles are won and lost out in the great nothingness of interstellar space.

spinning-top

The spinning-top comes with a passport. The traditional German model is fashioned of hollow wood and makes a vibrating sound as it spins. The French variety is pear-shaped, while the Spanish one dispenses with the upper point. But children born since the thirties no longer have spinning-tops made of wood. They have large tin narrow-side-down cones with rounded bases. They spin on a spiral rod which starts at the bottom as a single central foot and goes right through the top with a handle attached to its upper end, which is a miniature wooden version of the whole top. This smooth warm handle fills the little palm that grasps it. And the iron rod has to be very well greased because a child of three or four needs a lot of tries before he knows just the correct amount of pressure to apply to the interior mechanism to get the top to spin properly. So one persevered, pushing the handle up and down, spinning the top into a swirling crescendo until one could let it twirl off of its own accord across the floor. Then it would slow down and tumble over, still turning, while the coloured designs took on recognisable shapes out of the blurred movement of blue, red and yellow lines all mixed together.

That clanking noise was really incredible, it was as if its insides were self-destructing every time. And the power of the top's response to a hand start seemed to come from some independent creature within, screened by some exterior force, that was determined to remain hidden until the time came when it could emerge and liberate itself from its toyhood. All toys are a bit like that, careful liars sworn to keeping still and quiet, cunning vampires shamming away, who spy on children in the night so they can filch fragments of life from them.

swing

A smooth wooden plank which gently caressed the thighs. A thick rope which went through holes on either side and then tied onto a branch of the fig tree or a column of the pergola. In the end your hands got raw from gripping the two ropes at the top and had to be held open and blown on. Push faster and see the sky come closer. Swing higher, far from the ground. Up ahead, the Heavens. Down there, the Earth.

Legend tells us that Erigone, despairing daughter of Icarius, King of Laconia, hanged herself and that the shepherds who had killed her father, to absolve themselves, introduced a game as an everlasting memorial to her: the game of the rope hung in the trees. So the rocking of the swing is really the sinister oscillation of the hanged, the pendulum's rhythm, the coming and going of time. And the aerial death of Erigone brings to mind another myth, the unhappy flight of Icarus (no relation to Icarius), whose wings came apart in the sun.

Perhaps the swing embodies nostalgia for the cradle; but also the desire to escape it, to gain one's freedom. A small child is hurtled into space, on its own and against all the laws of gravity. A brave and hardy youngster on its celestial throne, in search of other worlds.... The exhausting acceleration of the climb which turns into pure speed. The side-drift of deceleration. And coming down on the

move, a dirt landing on unsteady legs that are still in flight.
A moment of surprise as your feet test out the ground – so
hard after the clouds.

tamburello

Your hand goes through the leather strap and your fingers grip the tamburello (a tambourine without chimes, used for ball games) by its wooden hoop. With little upwards jerks you get a small rubber ball to bounce on its taut diaphragm. Your eyes attentively follow the bounces with quick movements, up/down down/up, while your lips count in a barely audible whisper. The ball makes a pleasant rhythmic thunking. If you lose the rhythm the sound falls into gloomy discords, the bounce slows down and the ball takes a short swerve across the drum then falls to the ground. That's the tamburello game you can play on your own. It's an endurance test, a sort of training for the other game, something like tennis, that's played with a partner.

Face to face, three metres apart. Here the thunking is sharper, there's a long break between the thunk on one tamburello and the thunk on the other. The nice thing is that you're not playing against each other, the object isn't to get your partner to make a mistake but to get as many thunks as possible together. Perhaps because of this constructive aspect girls are best at tamburello. The players exchange beats on the beach in harmonious sets, feet burrowing in the sand in search of that underlying refreshing dampness. The boys however go for a more acrobatic sort of play, leaping, lobbing, hurling their dead weight against the ball, kicking up a dusty cloud, constantly breaking the rhythm...more like tennis or ping-pong.

Once upon a time courting couples happily played tamburello together and you would see the young men, stiff in those too-high bathing costumes, favour their graceful lady companions with the odd pointer, between one thunk and another.

teddy bear

It must be the roundness of its head. I don't know at what age you begin to appreciate it. Perhaps even in your cradle days. But above all it's the teddy bear's eyes that are so lovable. Sad and round, they seem so faithful, so docile. They say that babies like round shapes the best, and in fact this is a toy that keeps you company under the blankets, keeps you warm and protects you, but by the same token, he pleads, with his sorrowful expression, for warmth and comfort himself. The teddy is a sleepy, clumsy sort of creature. He doesn't have any fingers – just long delicately embroidered threads that suggest the contours of a hand, and just the rounded hint of a pink foot. At least that's how they were during a 1950's childhood. Today the range is slightly wider. But the march of progress in the teddy bear department has meant a return towards an even more perfect simplicity. Today's teddies don't have jointed arms and they're completely soft without any hard bits at all, even that stuck-out muzzle, even that nose, is soft. And they don't have pretend fingers done in embroidered wool; they're happy with their endearing little clawless stumps. They have ever-open arms and hands that don't grip. Although always ready to be cuddled, they don't hold on to you or imprison you. They're the most affectionate of all toys. Neither intrusive nor possessive. Their eyes, big and dark, tend to get lost in their fur. You have to search

for them by poking openings in the fur and as soon as your
hand is gone they disappear again, demonstrating a dis-
creet and courteous bashfulness. The most lovable teddies
have close-set eyes, as do especially sensitive people: eyes
almost rooted to the nose. Usually they're very small eyes,
extremely mild and beautiful. Teddy bears' eyes have
another source of attraction: they only seem small because
they're buried deep in the fur. Actually they're the enormous eyes of a nocturnal creature. Perhaps sometimes
peoples' small eyes are really very big. They seem small
because they don't readily let you look at them, they get
easily hurt by others' intrusions and so defend themselves
behind the narrow gorge of the eyelashes.

   Teddy bears made from fabric are so intimate with
children that each retains its owner's smell. Amongst the
many teddy bears that populate a child's room, that child
will find his favourite one straight away. All he has to do
is sniff. The smell of a bear used to sleeping with his little
master is quite heady; it's the smell of that child and the
universal smell of all children. Basically it's a sweetish
musty sort of odour from long, slightly humid sleeps. No
flesh and blood animal, no human adult could possibly
have a smell like that. Only fleetingly – after having picked
up the furious body of a child in one's arms, a child who's
just woken up or thrown off the blankets deep in the night
and got cold and run through a dark house holding his bear
shakily by a paw and hid in the grownups' bed.

train set

When you reached the age at which you could tie your own shoe laces, even if only the easy way – making loops with the two laces before crossing them over – you began to appreciate model trains. They belonged to your big brothers, but Dad was needed every time for setting-up. Because of this, winter Sunday afternoons, everybody still in their Sunday best, were usually the times for playing with trains. The miniature houses climbing the papier-mâché hillsides, the black tracks, the points, the level crossings, all took up half a room. The engine with its two or more carriages would leave slowly, disappearing through tunnels, reappearing undaunted, making steady speed and a monotonous hum. It would stop at all the stations. These were painted dark grey and green. The play consisted mainly of following the train with your eyes as it wove in and out of shadows cast by the window shutters, closed so that only the little way-lights of the train would show. It was a night transit train, with a contagious sense of calmness about it. One grew to adore it as one would a doll. Not because of its fine styling or the perfect attention to detail with which it imitated some original full-sized loco the grownups liked to refer to; but because of its liveliness, its capacity for movement, the way it conscientiously devoured the miles, sturdily thrusting into the night with its hidden load of trustfully slumbering passengers. And for

its lightness which one sensed was really a heaviness, and
for the encouraging prophecy about the hoped for/feared
for future that one could detect – straining one's ears – in
its candid rattle and clank.

view master

Today these live on only as holiday souvenirs, got up as fake snapshot or movie cameras. But the View Master, as one notes from the important-sounding name, a name as vanished from view as the object it names, was a toy in its own right which displayed beautiful images of both the real world and the world of fantasy and imagination, quite independently of where it was bought. It was a sort of rather solidly made pair of black binoculars. The two telescopes weren't the usual cylindrical shape but oblongs with a little circular lens closing the end. Seen from the front these lenses seemed like the thick specs of someone who was half blind. The View Master was really rather hideous to look at. But as soon as you inserted the cardboard disc – on which minute transparencies were mounted – and put your eyes to the eyepieces a wonderful scene appeared, space shrank and your field of view was completely filled with characters from fairy tales or the Churches of Florence or the Leaning Tower of Pisa or Venetian Gondolas or Tower Bridge or the Eiffel Tower or the Colosseum. A little lever on the side turned the disc and with every click another photo appeared until you went full circle back to the first picture. It was a cinema for movies that didn't move where you could watch, again and again to the point of nausea or until your arms ached or your eyes started to feel sore and your vision blurred, the silent version of 'Snow White' or 'Cinderella' or 'Sights of Italy' or 'The Wonderful World of Animals'. Not that the show itself was thought of as incredibly entertaining. It was the whole operation, slightly laborious and therefore very pleasurable: choosing your disc, inserting it into the little mechanism, and, above all, the clunk – as precise and resonant as a rifle shot or the click of a camera shutter – produced by the sturdy little lever on the side which you could depress as many times as you liked changing speed until the finger employed, which was always the index finger, got completely worn-out.

violante's wardrobe

In the childrens' newspaper there lived a certain 'Violante', a young girl, slim and blonde, who a few years later on would be called 'swinging'. She had long legs, straight as broomsticks, always flung apart in a run under her short skirt, a shoulder bag dangling precariously on one side, and white socks that barely reached her ankles. No memory lingers of the stories about her. They didn't strike the imagination and the mind didn't retain them. They weren't in rhyme. They weren't clever, ironic or even entertaining – they just gave a fairly realistic picture of the life of a girl between seven and twelve years old, struggling with her schoolwork, visiting her Granny, going on holidays near the seaside or up in the mountains. The weekly date with the little newspaper was terribly important, an emotionally fixed point. And in the children's paper there was Violante, with her horrid but unique name. Or was it her surname you asked yourself and went and looked it up for possible meanings; a kind of violet, a creature that could fly (*volare*) or a violent child? You never got used to that name – every time it stirred up feelings that would shift from hostility to affection.

Now and again Violante would appear in her vest and knickers. All around her spread over a whole page were drawings of clothes and accessories, trousers, scarves, berets if she was leaving for the mountains; bikinis, clogs,

and beachwear if she was off to the seaside. One was
supposed to stick the page onto stiff card but you could
never lay your hands on any fresh card and you used what
there was: cardboard from a shoe box, the liner from a pair
of stockings, the cover from an exercise book, a postcard,
the remains of an old sheet of card. This recycled card was
never enough for all the drawings so the only one that had
a card backing was Violante in her knickers. One cut the
designs out one by one, being ever so careful with the
edges. Each picture had white rectangles at the shoulders
and at the sides which would be folded around the figure
of the model so she could wear her wardrobe. It was tiring,
tricky work which took a few days to do. Sometimes the
scissors would slip and chop off one of the rectangles
making the item of clothing or accessory unusable. After a
while your thumb and index finger would start to hurt
where the handle of the scissors (the big pair or the little
pair, they always asked you why you wanted them) pressed
against your skin. They'd leave two purple marks on your
strained hand. You had boxes full of clothes for every
occasion and these became a sort of treasure, regarded with
envy by friends who weren't as patient. Inspired by this
wealth of different outfits you would make up stories
related to the life-style and personality of Violante that you
would spin out one after the other more or less as you would
do a few years later with your Barbie doll.

It seemed as if boys were never very fond of cutting
things out. Cutting out clothes at least: and for sure they
weren't interested in the strange pleasure of picking up
clothes with a moistened finger to lay them on a little
cardboard doll.

water pistol

Sometimes as you squirted away you got the urge to accompany the action with a sound, the sound the tongue makes if pressed up against the incisors and molars while discharging little spit balls. Similar to the noise of gas fizzing out when you uncork a bottle and you feel the release of excess energy. Even after being scolded by adults you still couldn't manage to restrain your tongue which, once it started, became quite unstoppable.

The water pistol would miraculously appear on the beaches and in the parks in the summertime because it was somehow associated with strong sunlight, that blinding whiteness that kills all other colours. Then in winter it would disappear again and it wouldn't occur to anyone to look for it. It was a light transparent thing. You'd fill it up gradually with a trickle of water and push the rubber stopper into the hole and take off for a preselected target. You'd shoot haphazardly, content with squirtability, never mind with hitting the target. A great lark: shoot yourself in the mouth and tickle your throat with the spray, refreshing yourself at this improvised fountain.

whistle

It was a very common thing to acquire a whistle at the fun-fair lucky dip. Maybe it was an easy shape for the crane to grasp when you manoeuvred it. Spread out on a bed of pebbles inside a glass box were all sorts of little toys – pipes, whistles, model cars and marbles. A mechanical arm with pincers at the end was controlled by a steering wheel. Drop a coin into the slot and the crane would start up, moving up and down and back and forth. At a certain moment its beak would open and shut again at great speed. If you knew how to steer it well you'd end up with a toy, otherwise just a handful of pebbles.

The metal whistle generally has the shape of a snail, while the wooden sort is long and thin; plastic whistles can imitate either of these models. Each makes a shrill sound, playing a single note; a *La* in the case of the round whistle used to tune guitars. You whistle to express the unstoppable force of childish energy, the pride you have in yourself and your own lungs which seem to be straining at the leash inside your chest; because your head is spinning and all your thoughts are emptying out of it, because your cheeks are getting red and your eyes turning into big happy balloons. You should blow really hard and repetitively to be as obnoxious as possible and get the maximum effect. Pretend to be directing a flow of enraged traffic and try to drown out all the imaginary honking and hooting. Whistling is by its very nature rowdy, out of control and absolutely exhilarating. You stop either when you run out of breath or because of outside pressure.

The bird call was a special kind of whistle that belonged to the huntsmen in the family. The very best one was flat, circular, made of metal and belonged to Grandpa. Playing it one became a winged being. But it wasn't easy to produce a magical chirping sound good enough to fool the sparrows. Grandpa would blow delicately and, feeling rejuvenated, his Adam's apple would start to vibrate as if it were producing the flowing note unaided. You would automatically peek out of the window and search the sky for a flock sufficiently suicidal to fly in.

windmills and whirlers

Nobody's ever exactly gone off their head about this toy. Even so, any time the windmill-seller showed up in the piazza every kid wanted one. He was quite irresistible with his basket hung round his neck, filled with nuts, liquorice, balls, flags and the toy windmills, stuck into the wicker, which twirled in the air whistling riotously. Next to them flew bunches of balloons. At home the windmill soon got put away somewhere. As a last resort on boring days it could be fished out again for a few irritating minutes. You blew distractedly on the propeller, pushed it round with a finger, or held it out at arms length from a window with the stick of the whirler tight in your hand to measure the wind strength and recapture the happy whistling of the piazza. Sometimes mothers would use old whirlers to decorate the balcony. They would stick them into flowerpots between the geraniums and the nasturtiums which hung over the balustrade, one in each pot pointed in different directions so that each aimed into the air at a different angle. Passing by down below you got the impression of a greeting, that someone up there was waiting for you....

wobbly animals

'**W**obbly animals' have never had a proper name. Every child makes up his own. One will call them 'up-downs', another one 'animal dancers'. They have paws made of two little cylinders connected inside with strings which, vein-like, run through the body from head to tail. The strings extend beyond the feet to a cylindrical wooden base and are attached to a button. When you push the button at the bottom you compress a spring hidden inside the cylinder. The strings slacken and the little animal goes into all kinds of funny positions; nods yes and shakes no with its head, wags its tail, collapses completely onto itself. The zoo includes puppies, pussy-cats, sheep, but also a little Pinocchio. Grownups, good at holding the base between the index and middle fingers while pushing the button with their thumb, amuse the little ones with these agile puppets in an improvised play. Children use both hands. They spend hours trying to create unusual positions, shaking the puppets in frenzied dances, killing off and resuscitating Pinocchio or squeezing gently to move just the head or bend a paw. Nowadays very few children even know that these little animal dancers exist. It's difficult to want something that doesn't have a name. To the few shopkeepers who still sell them they're just numbered 'items'. The modern versions have substituted nylon

strings for cotton ones, the result being a rather unnatural
stiffness.

yo-yo

Around 1930 a toy was resurrected from the dead. It took the lighthearted name of 'yo-yo' and became a classic. The children of Ancient Greece had played with it. During the French Revolution they yo-yoed the whole time, adults and all. But in those days it was called *émigrette*. Perhaps because it never stood still, perhaps after the nostalgia of southerners transplanted to the north and vice-versa. The Coblenz game or the emigrant's game; two wooden discs joined at the middle and separated by a deep furrow. A cord of vari-coloured threads woven together wraps and unwraps itself around the dowel pin that joins the two halves. You throw the yo-yo out with one hand while keeping the top end of the cord looped around the middle finger. After the yo-yo completes its descent it spontaneously changes direction reeling itself back up the still taut cord. If your hand can maintain the right rhythm the yo-yo will wind up and down either slowly or quickly at your behest. It's all a matter of having a sense of harmony and rhythm, an instinctive feel for music and movement. One doesn't learn to yo-yo – you get it straightaway or never at all, after that you just perfect your performance. So who yo-yos yo-yos and the others stand and watch.

Zoo

The carved wooden pony with its painted saddle on its base with four sky blue wheels went back and forth. Push down on the feet of the little white goose, a hatch opens in her belly and she lays some eggs for you. There was a crouching tiger with emerald green irises and pupils as narrow as grains of wild rice. And more geese, all shapes and sizes for floating around in the washbasin or dunking in the water. And a thick-maned Lion King, Lord of the Jungle, with a second trail of longer hairs running down his stomach, a tail furnished with a fine tuft of the same at its very end, a nose embroidered in rose-pink wool and large brown eyes. It goes without saying there was a bear too – all golden-brown. And a monkey who played the cymbals. These faithful sentries of sleep kept watch through the night, peering into the huge shadows flung out from a cloth-draped lamp. Christ on his crucifix seemed almost to breathe and ought at any moment start to speak like in the film *Marcellino, Pane e Vino*. In the framed picture he was dressed in blue and pointed to a large red heart beating away on the front of his garment. Underneath was written, 'Blessed heart of Jesus make me adore thee more with each day, blessed heart of Mary bring me unto salvation.' A tin globe made the shadow of a gigantic breast on the wall. The pendulum clock on the stairs (that was where the kid goat in the story of 'The Seven Little

Goats' hid from the hungry wolf) chimed the hours and half hours. Midnight – Cinderella's midnight – and real chimes merged with dream chimes counted by someone on the threshold of sleep who was trying to catch a certain Morpheus in the act of sprinkling golden dream-dust into cheekily still-open eyes.

DRAGONS... by Caio Fernando Abreu

The city of Sao Paolo, Brazil; fires
burn along the street in honour of the
god Shango and youngsters succumb
to mysterious diseases, a solitary male
cruising a bar realises he's become the
oldest customer, a man and a woman
sink together in a sea of love at a
kitsch Brazilian Hawaii while an
abandoned mistress seeks a last thrill
slipping into the red shoes. . .

*"Caio F. is not a pretentious writer
replete with pat solutions. His pieces end
abruptly; more like the itineraries of real
life, that lack the neat outcomes of TV
soaps."*
O JORNAL DO BRASIL

Boulevard Latin American series.
150 pages £5.95
ISBN 0 946889 22 8

Boulevard books are published in the
UK with Olive Press/Impact Books
and distributed by Harraps
Publishing Group.